THE BOY WITH A POUND IN HIS POCKET

THE BOY WITH A POUND IN HIS POCKET

A sister's fight for justice for her little brother

By JADE AKOUM

MIRROR BOOKS

MIRROR BOOKS

© Jade Akoum

1

Published in Great Britain and Ireland in 2022 by
Mirror Books, a Reach PLC business,
5 St Paul's Square, Liverpool, L3 9SJ.

www.mirrorbooks.co.uk
@TheMirrorBooks

Print ISBN: 9781913406929
eBook ISBN: 9781913406936

Illustrations acknowledgements:
Jade Akoum, Alamy, Reach Plc.

Page design and typesetting by Danny Lyle.

Printed and bound in Great Britain by
CPI Group (UK) Ltd, Croydon, CR0 4YY.

To my mum, Debbie,
and my brother, Yousef

PROLOGUE

"Mummy!"

A little hand tugs on mine, a voice as innocent as it is insistent.

"Mummy, can I speak? I want to talk about Uncle Yo-Yo."

"Oh, no darling," I say, my eyes swimming with tears. "Now's not the time."

But then I look at the faces around me, over 300 of them: politicians, community leaders, celebrities. And, most importantly, families. Ordinary decent families who are outraged and appalled by the idea that it might be possible to buy your way through the British justice system. They are here to support us. They are here to give Yousef a voice. My Yousef, my brother; the boy from the council estate with the pound coin in his pocket. He did not stand a chance against the wealth and privilege which brought him down.

And I realise it is *exactly* the right time.

I watch, my heart simultaneously breaking and bursting with pride, as my ten year-old son, Raafat, climbs onto the makeshift stage and takes the megaphone in his hands. He's not even strong enough to hold it, and, as it wobbles and the crowd holds a collective breath, my husband runs on stage to help him out.

Raafat looks out across the sea of faces, his small face tight with grief, anger and determination. And in him, suddenly, I can see hope. It shines like golden strands of gossamer, way ahead; too far for me to reach out and touch. But I know it's there. And in that moment, I know I can fight this.

"Justice for Yousef Makki!" he shouts, his tiny voice carrying across the courthouse square and beyond, into the city centre. "Justice for my uncle!"

1

"Finished!" shouted a little voice from upstairs, and I took the stairs, two at a time, straight into the bathroom.

There was my little brother, Yousef, sitting on the toilet, swinging his short legs, and reading *The Guardian*. It made me laugh every time. Yousef was only three years old and not yet big enough to pull his trousers up after going to the loo. Yet he was able to read a broadsheet newspaper to pass the time!

"Come on," I giggled. "Let's get these trousers up and I'll give you a piggy-back downstairs. Your tea's nearly ready."

Yousef was the baby brother I had always longed for, yet never dreamed I would ever actually get. For many years, it had just been my mum, Debbie, my older sister, Rachel, and me. We were happy enough, the three of us. But I was a tomboy; I loved playing football and climbing trees with my friends and then coming home full of mud and tales of my latest scrape.

"I want a baby brother to play with please," I told Mum.

"It doesn't really work like that. I'd need a boyfriend first," she laughed. "Anyway, I think you two girls are quite enough for me."

In 1996, soon after my sixth birthday, Mum met and married her first husband, an American. And it was decided after the wedding that we would go and live in Sugarland, Texas, near to his family home. For me, the change was tumultuous. I might as well have been moving to Mars. We went from a small council house in inner-city Manchester with shared bedrooms and a dingy back yard to a Texan mansion with our very own kidney-shaped swimming pool. Rachel and I could hardly believe it.

"A pool!" we shrieked. "And it's free? We don't need to pay?"

It should have been the start of a new and exciting chapter, but instead, all I could think of, as we sunbathed on our loungers, was the life I'd left behind. I missed riding my bike in the drizzle, on our grey Manchester street. I missed joking and squabbling with my mates on our way to school. I missed the penny sweets and my Nana's home-made custard and chocolate cake. I missed it all. And in Texas, everyone laughed at my accent too. I had to repeat everything I said two or three times. In school, I became the accidental and reluctant centre of attention. And though the other kids probably didn't mean any harm, I cringed with embarrassment. I was already a self-conscious child, and this just made me even worse. I was the outsider, the intruder, and I just didn't fit in. I couldn't see a way around it. One morning, two years on, without any warning, we found ourselves scurrying out of the house, chivvied along by Mum, in what seemed to me to be a thrilling top-secret mission.

"Just grab your shoes and coats and one toy each," she whispered. "Hurry girls, quick as you can."

I was breathless with excitement. I didn't care about the toys or the kidney-shaped swimming pool or the huge plush bedroom I was leaving behind. We took a bus to the nearest airport and later that same day, we were on a plane back home. I was too young to understand that Mum was deeply unhappy, and that we had walked out of our American dream with just the clothes we were wearing for a very good reason.

"I promise it will be fine," she told us, as we walked out onto the tarmac ready to board our plane. "I'm sorry girls but we just couldn't stay there any longer."

For me, she had no need to apologise at all. I couldn't wait to go home! Back in Manchester, we were allocated emergency accommodation by the council; a tiny two bed-roomed house, riddled with damp and even a family of mice for company, which I was very fond of, Mum markedly less so. Rachel and I shared a room with just a set of bunk beds inside and little else. It was cramped and noisy and the smells of the former occupants seemed to seep out of the walls themselves. But I didn't care one bit.

"It's just so good to be home," I beamed.

In time, we got a small rented house with a tiny backyard. Mum worked two jobs, as a nurse at night and hairdressing during the day. Our maternal grandmother, Nana Elsie, helped out with child-care. Elsie had been very strict with her own children, but with us, she was generous, indulgent and endlessly patient, shopping all over Manchester to find the right strawberry jam we liked and cutting our toast into dainty triangles.

"I didn't get the royal treatment when I was your age," Mum huffed, but her eyes were smiling; she loved that bond we shared with Nana.

Despite working long hours, Mum struggled to make ends meet; she had two children to raise on her own, after all. But I'd already learned that money did not make me happy. Just having my family and friends around me, with the security and familiarity of my own home and my own street; that was more than enough for me. I spent many blissful hours at weekends playing 'kerby' in the street with a football or fixing my bike ready to meet up with my pals. It was usually raining, often chilly, and there was rarely money for treats or new clothes. But I didn't worry about that. I was a real tomboy, a football fanatic, and I went on to have trials with both Manchester City and my beloved Manchester United. I lived for the training sessions and the weekend matches, and though I didn't make it through the academy, my love of the sport remained strong. I was settled and secure and content. I had – almost – everything I needed. For I longed, still, for a little brother.

"Either a brother, or a Labrador puppy?" I asked Mum. "Please?"

Either would have been marvellous.

"No chance, on both counts," she replied smartly.

One night, she decided to treat us to a rare meal out. It was probably a treat of some kind; perhaps a Friday night wind-down after a hard week at work. We lived in Rusholme, a district of Manchester famous for restaurants and cafés and we were spoilt for choice. Rachel and I changed our minds many times as we walked up and down Curry Mile, our noses pressed against the restaurant windows, taking in the rich smells and tastes osmotically. We weren't usually allowed out after dark, and it was mesmerising to see the neon lights and flashing signs and hear the sales pitches booming from the restaurant doors. It was enough of a night out for me just to walk down the street! Eventually, we ended up in a Mediterranean restaurant, where, as we were ordering, Mum got chatting to the chef, Ghaleb Makki.

They must have exchanged names and numbers because soon afterwards, he and Mum began dating. Ghaleb became a regular figure in our lives, over those coming months, and I grew to love him. He was a law student, originally from Lebanon, working as a chef in the evenings, to pay for his studies. He was two years younger than Mum. As a little girl, I remember being dazzled by the whiteness of his teeth and wondering how many times a day he brushed them. He was always smartly dressed too, impeccably groomed, and I was impressed by his suit and tie and his polished shoes. More importantly, he was kind and generous towards me and Rachel. He took us for days out and showed a real interest in our schoolwork. He was even a football fan. I began calling him 'Dad' and he slotted perfectly into our family, as though we'd been waiting for him to come along all these years. Ghaleb was Muslim, as were many of my school friends, and I was curious to learn more about the religion.

"I can teach you," Ghaleb offered. "Sure."

He lent me some books, and I went along to a talk too, at the public library. Mum was Roman Catholic, but she was a very peaceful and accepting person and open to me making my own choices.

"I'm happy with whatever makes you happy," she told me. "If you'd like to become Muslim, that's fine by me."

She and Ghaleb were married in a small Islamic ceremony early in 2000. Just a few months later, towards the autumn of 2000, Mum announced that she was pregnant. We all danced around the kitchen in celebration, and we couldn't wait for the new baby to come. But at just eight weeks, she suffered a miscarriage. It was devastating; all the more because it was so unexpected. Mum and I wept together after she broke the news. Though I was only ten years old, Mum confided in me, almost like a best friend. By nature, she was a very candid and open person, and not at all the sort to keep secrets, even from, or perhaps especially from, her young daughter. But more than that, we were extremely close; intertwined almost. Even as a child, I could sense when she had something on her mind, just as she could with me.

"When I'm feeling better, we'll try for another baby," she promised.

Early in 2001, she began to feel sickly and unwell. She made a GP appointment, and I went along with her after school.

"I think you're pregnant," the doctor told her. "Congratulations!"

Again, I was over the moon, but Mum, understandably, was more cautious.

"Let's leave it until we reach 12 weeks before we tell anyone outside the family," she decided.

It was an anxious wait but as time went on, and the weeks clicked by, we began to relax. I was allowed time off school to attend the scans, and my excitement, by now, was frothing over.

"Hope it's a boy, hope it's a boy," I said, hopping from one foot to the other.

When a nurse confirmed that Mum was indeed carrying a baby son, and I saw his tiny form wriggling on the monitor, I whooped with jubilation. It felt as though all my wishes had come true.

"Yes! At last!" I yelled, both hands in the air, and the nurse burst out laughing.

Mum's pregnancy was classed as high risk; she'd suffered an earlier miscarriage, she was also carrying a lot of fluid around the baby, and at 36, she was categorised as an older mum too.

"Take it easy," the midwife warned her.

I took the advice seriously. I pampered Mum all the way through those final months and tried to make sure she put her feet up every night, after work. The pregnancy was a learning curve for me; I grew up and became more independent during that time. Instead of relying on Mum to make me a packed lunch or pack my PE kit, I realised I could just as easily do it myself. She relied on me to pop to the shops for milk or to iron the odd school shirt and I thrived on the responsibility.

"I want to help," I insisted. "This is my baby brother, after all."

Rachel and I had different dads, and over that summer, she went to stay with her father in Devon. It was initially supposed to be for a short visit, but she ended up staying for much longer than planned. So, with Ghaleb working most evenings in the restaurant, that just left me and Mum at home. I cherished those times; the two of us curled up on the sofa, my feet in her lap, as we watched old musicals on TV. Mum loved anything she could sing along to! Sometimes, if the baby was awake, we'd see him kicking and stretching, and Mum's belly would pop out of shape. I was fascinated.

"I can't wait for him to arrive," I said longingly.

Mid-September, a month before the baby was due, Mum was admitted to St Mary's Hospital, Manchester, for monitoring. I was packed off to stay with Nana Elsie, because Ghaleb was working long hours, ready for the baby coming. Each day, I'd run home after school, desperate for news.

"Has she had him yet? Is he here?"

The wait was unbearable. It went on for ten days, and I refused to play out with my pals or even take a long bath, in case I missed a vital development. I resented even having to go to school each day. My mind was definitely elsewhere in lessons. Finally, Mum was booked in for a caesarean section. On September 28, 2001, I arrived home from school and as I got through the front door, Nana said to me:

"Keep your coat on, we're going to meet your baby brother!"

I flung my schoolbag down and off we went. We were so excited, we couldn't even wait for the bus to take us to the hospital, so we hailed a black cab. Nana wasn't in good health; she'd had her left leg amputated and lost her right eye too, after a battle with MRSA the previous year. But she scurried out of the house faster than I'd ever seen her move, and we flung her wheelchair into the back of the taxi as though we were Olympic athletes.

"To St Mary's!" I shrieked. "We're off to meet my baby brother!"

It felt like such a big adventure. And in the maternity wing, when I caught the first glimpse of baby Yousef Ghaleb Makki, my heart spilled over with joy. He was more beautiful, more precious, than I could ever have imagined. Despite being two weeks early, he weighed a bouncing 9lbs and he was perfect in every way; liquid brown eyes and masses of dark hair.

"Is he real?" I asked Mum, in awe. "Is he ours? Are we actually taking this baby home?"

I was beside myself. I had never felt love like it and a small part of me was panicking that this might not be genuine, that he might not be ours to keep after all. It felt too good to be true.

"He's ours, don't worry," Mum said. "He looks just like you, I think."

And she was right; I could see it too. My skin was fair, and my hair was lighter, but we had the same sort of mouth and the same almond-shaped eyes. He even had the little crinkle under his eyes, just like me. I was so proud. When I walked out of the hospital that evening, my feet barely touched the floor. I was suspended in a cloud of pure happiness.

2

When baby Yousef came home, I insisted on helping out with the nappy changes and the bottle feeds. I loved folding the baby-gros and the tiny white vests and marvelling at the size of his scratch mitts and his miniature socks. Even during the night, I'd wake, automatically, as he began to murmur, and creep into Mum's room to help.

"You should be asleep, Jade," she whispered. "You'll never get up for school in the morning!"

But she loved me fussing around him, I could tell. She called me his 'little mother hen' and I wrapped the nickname around me like a blanket, soft and snug.

"Pass me the wipes, mother hen," she'd smile. "And a new nappy too please."

And after he was fed and winded and changed, and back in his cot, I was the one who lulled baby Yousef back to sleep with my rendition of 'Twinkle Twinkle' or 'You Are My Sunshine.' When his big eyes locked with mine, I felt I could see right into his future. And I knew he was going to be someone.

"You really are my sunshine," I told him gently, before I slipped quietly back into my own bed.

When I turned up a few moments late at school the next morning, bleary-eyed and tired, I felt a flash of envy from all my friends. Everyone wanted a little brother like mine, everyone wanted to be called upon to sing night-time lullabies, and I felt as though I'd won the biggest prize. I was the one with the baby brother! I was the one with the dream come true!

More than anything, I loved to watch Yousef sleep; the way his dark eyelashes rested softly on his cheek, and his plump little fingers curled around his blanket.

"You're going to break some hearts," I told him. "You're like a little king."

And for those first few months, Yousef's nickname was 'King.' To us, that's who he was. The centre of our world. He was so wanted, so adored. And when everyone said I was like a second mummy to him, it was the best compliment I could have had. I'd started high school just a couple of weeks before he was born, so it was a busy time, full of new experiences. And though I loved my new classes and my new friends, I hated leaving Yousef every day.

"Let me stay off school," I begged Mum. "I'd rather look after Yousef with you."

Part of me wanted to walk home after school with my pals and savour my new independence. But a bigger part of me wanted Mum to meet me at the school gates, so that I could show my baby brother off to my friends.

"He's gorgeous," they cooed. "You're so lucky Jade."

I puffed out with pride, pushing the pram home, alongside Mum. I would look back on those months as the best time of my entire childhood. In September 2002, we flew out to Saida, Lebanon, to visit Ghaleb's relatives there. They had never met Yousef before and so it was a grand occasion. The whole family was so welcoming and friendly, making us feel instantly at home. But I made one friendship during that holiday that was infinitely more special than the rest. Mazen Akoum was 15 years old, over three years older than me. He lived on the same street as Ghaleb's family and his English was good, so he was often called round to the house to act as unofficial translator. The moment I saw him, I was transfixed. He was so handsome!

"I didn't know they had boys like that round here," I told Mum later. "I'm going to marry him when I grow up. You wait and see."

She rolled her eyes, and it became something of a private joke between us, during our nine-day holiday.

"I think you'll change your mind before then," she smiled.

"I'll marry him," I insisted. "He's the boy for me."

Yousef turned one whilst we were in Lebanon and Ghaleb's family threw a huge party for him and made him a Mickey Mouse birthday cake. I still have the single candle from his cake to this day. Back then, I could never have known how precious it would become. Part-way through our stay, Yousef took his first, wobbly steps in the sunshine of Saida, and we all applauded so loudly that he burst into tears and fell over back on the floor again. I was the first to scoop him into my arms and soothe his tears.

"You're a clever boy! Walking aged one!" I cooed.

Saida was a lovely city, a tourist hot spot with a castle at its centre, and beautiful beaches along the coastline. There were many vibrant and bustling markets and a wide choice of restaurants too. I was glad that Mazen appointed himself as our guide, to show us around and I got the feeling that he liked me, too. On our final day, as we packed our bags ready for the airport, I invented as many complex conversations as I could, so that Mazen had to be summoned to translate. When it was time for the final goodbye, we exchanged numbers and promised to keep in touch.

"I'll miss you," he told me shyly.

"Me too," I replied.

In my mind, I knew it was only a matter of time until I saw him again, only a matter of time until I walked down the aisle with him.

3

Back at home in Manchester, Yousef grew into a lively toddler, full of mischief. His nickname changed from 'King' to 'Yo-Yo' because he was constantly on the move, bobbing up and down as though he was battery operated.

Towards the end of 2002, Mum and Ghaleb began arguing, mainly over money worries, and in the spring of 2003 they decided to have a temporary break from one another. Ghaleb moved out, leaving just Mum, me and Yousef at home. As a pick-me-up, Mum took us to Blackpool for the weekend. I'd been before, on annual holidays, and I loved showing Yousef the beach and the arcades and buying him his first ice-cream. As we walked down the promenade, we spotted a psychic's tent, and Mum went in, just for fun.

"You're pregnant," the psychic told her.

"I very much doubt it," Mum giggled, but when we got home to Manchester, she did a pregnancy test, just out of curiosity.

"Jade!" she yelled, running out of the bathroom, waving the stick in the air. "You're not going to believe this! It's positive!"

The news was as exciting as it was surprising.

"Another baby!" I yelled. "Hope it's a boy! Cross your fingers for a boy, Mum!"

She and Ghaleb decided to give their relationship another go, and we looked forward to the birth of another new family member; another brother, if I had anything to do with it. In December 2003, my wishes came true and my second brother, Mazen, was born. We named him Maz, for short, and he was beautiful, so impossibly cute. I doted on both of my baby brothers. I was glad that, with two babies demanding attention, I could be hands-on and useful for Mum. I wanted to help her of course, but also, I loved the feeling of satisfaction I got from being helpful. I had always been that way; I thrived on being needed.

When Maz was three months old, Nana Elsie sadly passed away, aged 61, which hit us all hard, especially Mum. After more arguments, she and Ghaleb split again and over the summer of 2004, we found ourselves once more in a women's hostel in Stretford, Manchester. It was the start of a tough time. We all had to share the same poky room, with bunkbeds in the corner and a tatty travel cot jammed in by the side. There was a communal bathroom, kitchen, and TV lounge and though I was used to basic facilities, this place was eye-opening.

"Is this legal?" I asked Mum, and she smiled at my naivety.

"'Fraid so," she replied. "But it won't be forever, I promise you that."

Most of the other residents were like us; decent people going through a very bad period in their lives. But there was a predictable handful of troublemakers too who seemed hellbent on making everyone else's lives a misery. The weekends were the worst, because that was when the hostel staff went home and there was nobody left in charge. On Saturday nights there were often rows and even fights in the communal areas. We cowered in the bedroom, Mum's arms tight and reassuring around us, doors locked; half fascinated, half terrified by the wars raging outside our walls. We might as well have been prisoners. Night after night I lay awake, listening to the swearing and screaming in the corridors, worrying that they might break down the door and decide to pick on us next. And often, when Monday morning came, and it was time for school, I was reluctant to leave my little brothers behind at the mercy of the hostel's hell-raisers. I knew my fear wasn't rational; they were safe enough with Mum and though she would never have got involved in any of the trouble, she wouldn't have let anything happen to the boys either.

"I don't want you to miss school," Mum told me. "You mustn't fret about us."

But I was a born worrier. I couldn't help it. Despite Mum's protests, I occasionally skipped school, just to keep an eye on them and put my mind at rest. And also, it was two buses to school from the hostel, a tricky and convoluted journey, so a day off was nice sometimes.

"Come on boys!" I'd say. "We're having a day off! A little treat!"

I'd bump the double pram down the uncarpeted stairs and along the cluttered hallway in the hostel, ignoring the irate voices from behind closed doors. It was lovely just to escape outside, into the fresh air, with my baby brothers. Yousef by now was three years old and Mazen was nine months old. We'd go off to the park to feed the ducks or maybe to the local shopping centre so that Yousef could run up and down the shiny tiles and perform knee-slides.

"Are we going back to the Nasty House?" Yousef asked, when it was time for us to go back to the hostel.

The nickname stuck, and it pulled at my heartstrings. That's exactly what it was; he had summed it up perfectly. We all missed our neat semi, with the small patch of garden, our own toilet, and our own cooker. They were the simple, unsophisticated things which we had now learned never to take for granted. Yet no matter how bad things got, how frightened, or frustrated I felt, I never once wished I was back in Texas in the millionaire's mansion. That life just wasn't for me.

"We'll get out of this place soon," Mum promised me. "I'm doing my best."

She'd had to give up her nursing job, with two little ones to look after, so it was slow progress. But she saved what she could, and she was both resourceful and resilient. Yousef turned three that September, and despite our struggles, Mum went all out for his birthday. Even back then, I marvelled at how she did that, and I admired her for it too. No matter what happened, whether we were living in a mansion or a homeless hostel, us kids all had brilliant birthdays. They were fiercely non-negotiable days of fun, laughter and celebration. Having looked at the state of the oven in the shared kitchen, Mum opted to buy Yousef a birthday cake, and after the ceremonial blowing out of the candles, we went to the cinema and then on to McDonald's.

"That was the best birthday!" Yousef beamed, as I tucked him into bed that night.

After fifteen months in the hostel, Mum found us a new house, another rented semi, but this time with three bedrooms and a slightly bigger garden on a council estate in Burnage, Manchester. Ghaleb was around to help with the move, and despite their differences, he and Mum tried hard to remain friends. Sometimes, Yousef would refuse to sleep at night without his daddy, so Ghaleb would come round to read a bedtime story and settle him down. Life was good again and on an even keel; Mum went back to work, doing hospital night shifts and fitting in hairdressing jobs in-between the day-to-day challenges of motherhood. I was 15 by now and helping out more and more with baby-sitting too. But it was around this time that Mum began dropping things and losing her balance a little. At first, it was just the odd cup or plate whilst she was doing the dishes, or she'd maybe struggle with her co-ordination whilst she was carrying shopping bags. For a while, she just put it down to exhaustion or clumsiness.

"I need to pay more attention," she smiled ruefully, as she swept up yet another broken coffee cup from the kitchen floor.

But eventually, her GP referred her for tests, and she was later diagnosed with rheumatoid arthritis. It was a huge blow, she was told it was a serious and degenerative illness, but she was only 38 years old and determined to stay positive. The illness seemed to come in waves, and for weeks, she would be absolutely fine. But sometimes, without any warning, she struggled even to get out of bed. I was so glad I was there to help out with the two boys.

"I don't know what I'd do without you," she told me. "You're my little mother hen."

4

By the time 2005 came around, we were starting to notice there was something rather unusual about Yousef. Physically, he progressed quickly, hitting all his milestones, much sooner than we expected. He had sat up unaided before six months and had walked aged one in Lebanon. He was well-coordinated, agile and quick. But it was his mental development that left us stunned. He talked constantly, always asking questions, always challenging the answers. It was exhausting, just listening to him. When I took him out for a walk, he made childish and often comical attempts to read the street signs and the shop names as we passed. He was still only three years old, and though we read to him a lot at home, we hadn't started teaching him to read himself yet. He just seemed to pick it up, organically. It was mind boggling. He knew our address, including the postcode and he'd share it with most people he met. In the supermarket, people stopped and laughed as he sang out our door number and street name.

"He's a clever boy," they said.

Mum was a big reader and her enthusiasm had certainly rubbed off on me, and now on Yousef too. In the evenings, at bedtime, whilst Mum was busy settling baby Maz, I'd read Roald Dahl or Julia Donaldson stories to Yousef. His brown eyes were wide; rapt and spellbound. And it wasn't long before he was peering over my shoulder at the pages, and sounding out the text himself. He couldn't pronounce my name and so he called me: 'Chade' instead.

"What's this word, Chade?" he asked. "And this one? And can we read another book after this is finished?"

It wasn't lost on me, that though he couldn't say my name, he could read it. He was like a little sponge; the more I taught him, the more he wanted to know. He was learning to write too, scrawling a letter 'Y' in felt pen in his colouring book, or writing in chalk on the path outside. Around that time, it was on Mum's endless list of jobs to paint the garden wall in red. So before she did it, she allowed Yousef to write his name across the bricks with a marker pen. That was very typical of Mum; she was creative and imaginative and forever encouraging us to stretch our horizons and think outside of the ordinary. Yousef dashed out into the garden with his pencil case and wrote his name, over and over. When he had finished, it looked so cute, and he was so impressed by his own efforts that Mum couldn't bear to paint over his handiwork.

"I think I'll keep it, as a memory," she smiled.

In bed, Yousef liked to wear socks on his hands, as a comfort to lull him to sleep. Each hand had to have a different colour sock too, he never wore matching ones. Sometimes, he even wore his hand-socks around the house, along with his favourite Spiderman costume, complete with false muscles bulging on his arms. He'd dive off the furniture, projecting imaginary webs across the living room.

"Sit down, Yo-Yo," I was always telling him. "You'll tire yourself out."

But he could never sit still. He was always looking for his next adventure, his next challenge. He was filled with energy and fizz, but though he was inquisitive, he wasn't naughty or boisterous. And he was very gentle with baby Maz too; with just two years between them, they had a unique bond. As Maz became a toddler, they both shared a bedroom and got bunk beds; Yousef was in the top bunk with Maz underneath. It was a struggle each night to get the hand-socks and the suit off Yousef so we could throw them in the washing machine. He would have gone to bed as Spiderman if we'd let him! More often than not, when I went in to check on the boys before my own bedtime, they were both snuggled in the same bunk together, arms around each other. I'd often sit on the edge of the bed and watch them sleep, drinking in the picture of bliss before me. During the day, the two of them would team up to play pranks and tricks on us too. Maz was the mischief-maker and would carry a happily complicit Yousef along with him. One day, they squeezed an entire bottle of washing up liquid down the toilet and the bubbles flowed over the top of the bowl and onto the bathroom tiles. They thought it was hilarious.

"Boys!" yelled Mum in exasperation.

Another time, I found pasta in my school shoes. One morning, there was an egg in my shoe, and I'd put my foot in and cracked it before I noticed.

"Yousef! Maz!" I shouted. "You're in such big trouble now!"

But all I got in response were peals of laughter from the bunkbeds. One of their favourite jokes was to hide the house keys and then sit and giggle on the couch together as me and Mum frantically tore the entire house apart. They had a brilliant sense of fun. Maz loved pulling toys apart and Yousef liked to fix them again. He was always captivated by the way everything worked. For their birthdays, Mum would throw big parties in the house, with a bouncy castle in the back garden. All the local kids came. Yousef was one of a big crowd of children in our area and there was a strong feeling of community and togetherness. And yet, he was quite definitely one on his own too. He continued to amaze us academically, even though he hadn't yet started school. Like a little old man, he began taking *The Guardian* newspaper into the bathroom with him. It was a comical sight; his legs weren't yet long enough to reach the floor as he sat on the toilet, but he would quite happily attempt to read articles that some adults would struggle to understand. The newspaper itself was too big for him; it kept folding in and falling on him.

"You're a one-off," I told him.

Mum was studying for a promotion into psychiatric nursing and so there were often medical books lying around the house. To my amazement, Yousef started picking them up and reading them too. One day, I came home from school, and he turned to me, quite seriously, and said:

"Did you know babies only blink once or twice a minute but the average adult blinks about 10-15 times a minute?"

I was amazed. I didn't know what to say. Not many little boys had an in-depth knowledge of Biology. One of his favourite questions, just as I was tucking him into bed, was: "How was I made? Where did I come from? And if I came from Mummy, where did she come from?"

He made me sit on the bed and he listened patiently whilst I answered his questions the best I could, though many were beyond me. Of course I knew that the little boy in Yousef was putting off bedtime, stretching out the last few moments of his day. But another part of him was genuinely thirsty to learn.

"And what about the earth?" he demanded, as I flicked on his night-light. "Who made that?"

"Go to sleep," I said sternly, but I smiled to myself all the way down the stairs.

Before I went to bed, I folded his *Guardian* newspaper away in the bathroom, and I stacked up his medical books in the living room. From the moment he was born, I had always known Yousef was special. But now, I knew it was more than that. He was a boy who was going to change the world.

5

During the winter after Yousef's fourth birthday, it had snowed quite heavily, and Ghaleb took us all out in his silver Zafira to look at the neighbourhood snowmen. We loved going for drives; we'd play Whitney Houston, Celine Dion or Frank Sinatra, at full blast, and Yousef and I sang along at the tops of our voices; he knew all the words to all the cheesiest songs! After the snow, that particular after-noon, the roads were treacherous; sludgy and icy, and the car skidded a little on a corner.

"You shouldn't turn the wheel against the skid," piped up a little voice from the back seat. "And take your feet off the pedals!"

My jaw hung open in astonishment, and Ghaleb's did the same. Coming from Lebanon, he had no experience of driving in the snow, and this advice certainly hadn't come from him.

"How on earth do you know that?" I asked Yousef.

"I heard it somewhere," he replied proudly. "It was on the TV. I remember everything."

One evening, soon after, Ghaleb was visiting the boys, and playing the card game 'Patience' at the dining table. Yousef, forever full of questions, wanted to know what he was doing. I was watching TV, half-listening, as Ghaleb explained the differences between the red and the black cards, and the numbers on each card. Yousef was captivated. After the game was finished, Yousef collected the cards, one by one, face up, and put them in a pile facing down. Then, before he turned each one over, he shouted:

"Nine of clubs!"

"Queen of hearts!"

"Three of spades!"

Suddenly, I snapped to attention and realised that he was correctly predicting each card before he turned it over. He had memorised them all, as he was picking them up. I watched, transfixed, as he correctly named 17 cards, before finally making a mistake.

"Yousef!" I gulped. "Wow!"

But he just smiled and shrugged; pleased but a little baffled by our reactions. For him, really, it was no big deal.

In the summer of 2006, before he started school, Yousef's grandparents in Lebanon arranged for him to fly out to see him, accompanied by an uncle and a close family friend. Mum wasn't at all sure about the trip at first; Yousef had never been away from her, not even for a night, and she was worried about missing him – and him missing us too. Little Maz was still too young to travel, but when we asked Yousef if he wanted to go, he nodded excitedly.

"Ok. Just for one week," Mum agreed.

She knew that Ghaleb's family would take good care of him, but it was still a wrench for her. Yousef was so chuffed to be going on an aeroplane and visiting the other side of his family that it was hard not to be carried along with his enthusiasm. But he had barely been gone a day when reports came on the news of unrest in Lebanon. Then came a declaration that the country was unsafe. Mum was beside herself with panic. Ghaleb's family organised to have Yousef flown out of the country by helicopter to Cyprus, and arrangements were then made, with the foreign office, to fly him home as an emergency along with other British nationals. It was a frantic time. Mum and I barely slept in those hours, we were fraught with worry. Three days on, we received the instructions to meet Yousef at Manchester Airport, alongside the family members he had flown with. When they came through arrivals, and we saw his familiar little head bobbing in the crowd, Mum and I threw ourselves at him.

"We thought we might never see you again," I gasped. "You poor boy. Was it very scary?"

Yousef laughed.

"I didn't want to come home," he said. "I loved all the bangs and the lights in the sky. They told me they were fireworks, but I knew they were bombs. I just played along with the joke."

Mum took him firmly by the hand.

"You won't be travelling anywhere on your own again," she said resolutely. "You're not leaving Manchester from now on."

In September 2006, Yousef started primary school. All throughout August, he had been excitedly trying on his little blue jumper and his school shorts at least once a day. He just couldn't wait.

"You'll wear that uniform out before you even start at this rate," Mum chuckled.

His first day came around, and Mum, Ghaleb and I walked with him to Ladybarn Primary School, Manchester, with little Maz chattering away in the pram. At the school gates, there were the inevitable tears and tantrums from the children who didn't want to be separated from their parents for the first time. But Yousef gave us a cheery wave and walked into his classroom without looking back, as though it was just where he belonged.

"Bye, Yousef!" I called, but he had already gone.

And from then on, he welcomed education into his life as though it was his oxygen. He blossomed at school, enthusiastically and passionately soaking up knowledge and information. The only thing Yousef didn't like about school were the weekends.

"I don't like to miss my lessons," he told me. "I want to go every day."

Some Saturdays, he'd get up and put his uniform on, out of the laundry basket, as though he thought he could somehow trick us into taking him into school. By the first half-term holiday, in October, most of the other children were tired and ready for a break. But school just seemed to galvanise Yousef and fire him up to learn. The more he knew, the more he was energised. It was as though a one-way switch had been flicked in his mind, and he wanted to be taught more and more and more. It was almost a need in him; a healthy and insatiable addiction. When parents' evening came around, I went along with Mum to hear how he was doing.

"He's just marvellous," the teacher told us. "He's a nice, polite little boy and so keen and eager. My only concern is that his arm must get tired, because he has his hand up all of the time!"

On our way out of the parents' evening, a teacher stopped Mum and said to her:

"I'm sure you know how bright your son is. I would describe him as a 'once in a lifetime' pupil. We feel very lucky to have him here."

"We're very lucky to have you," Mum replied. "So, thank you. All of you."

At home, we encouraged him as much as we could. Mum bought him the 'Horrible Histories' book set and, after he had whizzed through those, Ghaleb presented him with a set of encyclopaedias. Yousef devoured every book, and soon he was teaching Mum and Ghaleb too.

"The structure of La Liga is different to that of the Premiership," he told Ghaleb. "Look. I'll show you why."

And another day:

"Did you know Richard the Lionheart refused to get married?"

One day, still in that first year of school, Ghaleb bought a computer home and Yousef and little Maz clustered around it, their stubby fingers pressing keys at random. At first, they played games on the CBeebies website or listened to stories. But then, Yousef began asking me to type searches into Google.

"Are there other universes beyond ours?"

"What's at the bottom of the sea?"

"How far away is the sun?"

He had a particular obsession with history and science. In the evenings, he loved to sit and watch documentaries, followed by long discussions afterwards. One night, we watched a programme on space and then I took him upstairs to bed and showed him the stars outside his bedroom window.

"How do the planets just hang there?" he asked curiously. "Why don't they fall down?"

I shook my head, simultaneously perplexed and impressed.

"I have no idea," I replied. "I'd never really thought about it."

Keen to be involved in his education, and to give something back, Mum volunteered to help out with his class and on her days off she would go into school to listen to the children reading. And when the school trips came around, she added her name to the list too.

"I've learned my lesson since the Lebanon holiday," she joked. "I won't let him out of my sight."

She and I even joined the parents' committee to help organise the school fairs and fundraising nights. Mum became such a well-known face around the school over the years. She channelled all of her energy into parenting. For her, there was no contest. Motherhood was unrivalled in terms of both challenge and of reward. I would later remember with such fondness the sacrifices and the efforts she made and do my best to replicate that for my own children.

As well as reading and learning, Yousef could apply himself practically too. By the age of five he could work pretty much every piece of equipment in the house. When the washing machine was on the blink, he crouched down, next to Mum, and gave her advice on how to fix it.

"Do you know," she said to me afterwards. "He didn't fix it, but his advice actually made pretty good sense."

He loved taking apart remote controls, or rusty old toasters and kettles, to see how they worked.

"Look at this!" he'd say, holding up an element and an old piece of wire. "This all makes sense to me now."

Ghaleb gave him simple algebra problems to do, and, after he was shown the method, he breezed through the entire list.

"Can't you give me more difficult ones?" he asked.

Ghaleb and Yousef loved watching 'Who Wants To Be A Millionaire?' on TV. They were both very competitive, shouting out the answers, desperate each to be the first. Ghaleb even applied to go on the show, just to make Yousef happy. But although he made 18 attempts to get through the selection process, he was never successful.

"I'll go on the show when I'm a grown-up," Yousef promised him. "And I will win a million pounds for us all."

"That wouldn't surprise me," Ghaleb winked.

Yousef carried around a little notebook and pen and was forever whipping it out to write down a new fact. If there was something he didn't understand, he would scribble it in his book and ask me to look it up later for him online. After his night-time bath, he'd often dash downstairs to check the names of the arteries to the heart, or the number of bones in the human body.

"There's the next Nobel prize winner, sitting right there," Mum chuckled, as Yousef ran through his list of questions, and I sang out the answers from Google.

Meanwhile, I had left school by now, and my plan was to work with young children. I was still keeping in touch with my friend, Mazen, in Lebanon. Sometimes, it might just be a couple of WhatsApp messages a day. Other times, we'd talk for hours on video call, and though we were from different cultures and distant countries, we never ran out of things to say.

"I'm going to marry him," I said again to Mum.

These days, she just inclined her head a little and smiled. She could see how well we got on, even though we were three thousand miles apart. We both knew this was much more than a holiday romance. And whilst my friends were fancying and dating local boys, I had no interest at all in anyone else except Mazen. I got a part-time job to save money for a plane ticket, and early in 2007, I flew out to Lebanon, taking little Maz, three, with me for a visit. I stayed with Ghaleb's family, who gave me a warm welcome and treated me just like a granddaughter. But of course the real purpose of my trip was to see Mazen who lived just down the road. By now, I was 16 and he was 20. He met me at the airport and my stomach flipped. He was every bit as gorgeous as I had remembered.

"I've really missed you," he said.

"Me too," I blushed.

The next day, we met up for a walk around the local markets and afterwards, in the ice-cream parlour, he held my hand under the table. I felt my heart racing. From that moment, we were never apart. We had days at the beach or at the shops, or he'd treat me to a nice restaurant, always with little Maz in tow. Maz was quite a shy little boy and didn't like me to leave him alone for a moment. He would cry if I left him with his grandparents. But Mazen was very patient and kind and didn't complain when Maz played gooseberry! Most teenage boys would have pulled a face at having a younger sibling tagging along, but not Mazen. I knew then that I had been right about him, and that he was the man for me.

Later in the week, Mazen's aunt, Desiree, announced that she had booked a salon for me to have my hair and nails done. Mazen's parents would look after little Maz, bribing him with a big ice-cream. It was all arranged.

"My treat," she smiled.

Her English was perfect, and she was very generous, but I couldn't help thinking there was something behind it. Mazen had been behaving oddly too that morning; furtive and a little on edge. When we got back to the house, he whisked me quickly through the dining room and into the bedroom. My entire body prickled with anticipation. I hoped that I'd guessed correctly what was coming next.

"Jade, please will you marry me?" he asked, dropping down onto one knee. "I want to spend the rest of my life with you."

"Yes!" I squealed. "Yes! Yes! Yes! I'll marry you!"

He presented me with a beautiful gold engagement ring, with a diamond centre, and I threw my arms around him. From outside the door came a big cheer, and I could hear little Maz whooping and shouting my name. Mazen's entire family had been eavesdropping! They had secretly prepared a party too, with cakes and balloons and banners.

"It's a good job I said yes," I winked at Mazen.

But really, though we were so young, we were completely sure of each other. There was never any doubt. Little Maz sat at the dining table, next to me, with his cheeks bulging with chocolate cake.

"I will marry you!" he kept repeating. "Yes! Yes! Yes!"

I felt so lucky, so at ease in this new family, who had embraced me and welcomed me as Mazen's fiancée. There were lots of tears as we said goodbye at the airport, but I knew that not long into the future, we would be getting married and be together for good. Back at home, I found a job in a children's nursery, Mazen worked hard in Lebanon, studying his biomedical engineering degree as well as working part-time, and we began saving for our next flight. It was a long-distance love affair but all the more intense for it.

In December 2007, I returned to Lebanon, with Mum, Yousef and Maz, for my wedding. Mum was recovering from recent arthritis surgery on her knees, so she was having difficulty walking. But she was determined to make the journey.

"I wouldn't miss it for the world," she told me.

Mazen's parents, Raafat and Joumana, had gone all out to make it a special day. They had ordered a seven-tier wedding cake and booked a plush venue near their home. Mum and I went shopping for a wedding dress and trailed from one bridal shop to another, before spotting the perfect dress. It was very traditional; an all-white, full-length gown with sparkling jewels sewn into the bodice and specks of glitter on the skirt. Mum's eyes filled with tears as I twirled around in the shop.

"Beautiful," she beamed. "That's the one. You look like a princess."

We couldn't afford to buy it and instead rented it just for the day. I couldn't wait to collect it. When the big day dawned, my stomach was doing nervous somersaults.

"Why are they taking you away?" Yousef asked, his little face screwed up with concern as I applied the finishing touches to my make-up. "Why can't you stay with us?"

"I won't ever leave you," I promised, kissing the top of his nose. "Nobody will ever take me away. Mazen is joining our family, so you're getting a new brother."

The ceremony itself was a little overwhelming; there were hundreds of people there and I felt awkward as the centre of attention. But when I caught Mazen's eye, and he took his hand in mine, I felt a surge of love and confidence. This man was my future. I had known it from the first moment we met. Afterwards, we spent a few days on honeymoon in a lovely hotel before it was time for me to fly home. Mazen wasn't allowed to come to the UK with me, because his visa had yet to be approved. And leaving him behind at the airport was heart-rending.

"We'll just have to keep visiting each other, until my visa comes through," he said. "It won't be long."

He had already been granted a student visa, as he was studying biomedical engineering in Lebanon and hoped to continue postgraduate qualifications in the UK. But after we got engaged, he had changed his application to a spousal visa, and, despite the fact that he was being completely honest and transparent, the authorities seemed to become unreasonably suspicious. The visa was refused, and we were advised to appeal. We were then asked to provide proof of our relationship; intimate letters, messages, photographs. We had lots of evidence, of course. But it felt so invasive, sharing our private thoughts and messages with complete strangers. And even then, that wasn't enough, and I was called in to attend a string of meetings with faceless bureaucrats in air-conditioned government buildings, to spill out the details of our love-life. It felt trashy and demeaning.

"We're absolutely, utterly, in love," I said, my palms open in front of me. "I don't know how else I can convince you."

Of course I understood that they wanted to check that our marriage was genuine. We had to follow the rules, just like everyone else. I had absolute confidence that, after our appeal was processed, we would be allowed to be together. Whilst the checks were ongoing, Mazen and I visited each other as often as we could. He had a part-time job fixing computers and he also helped out in his uncle's clothing business. I saved every penny I could from my part-time nursery work, and I received Education Maintenance Allowance from my childcare college course too. Mazen would often wire money over to me and his family was very supportive; his dad was a police officer and helped us out with costs and finding a good immigration solicitor for Mazen.

But the appeal dragged on and on. I even considered moving to Lebanon, to be with Mazen. His family had accepted and embraced me, and I knew I could be happy there. The weather was certainly an improvement on Manchester! It was a different culture of course, but I seemed to slot right in each time I visited. In addition to their home in the city, Mazen's family had a smaller place in the mountains, which was a 45-minute drive away. The first time I went there, I was spell-bound. Looking out from their balcony, over the lush green of the mountainside, I felt like I had walked straight into a scene from Disney's 'Aladdin'. It was such a magical place; it didn't feel real. In the mornings, when I awoke, there were donkeys and chickens causing a riot outside the windows. The pace of life there was slow and simple; unhurried and unconcerned.

"I love it here," I said dreamily.

Back in Saida, Mazen had noticed that I really missed some items of food from home, so he found a supermarket selling English tea-bags, HP sauce and Pop Tarts.

"Here," he said, handing me a bag of shopping. "This will put a smile on your face."

"It's like a home from home here," I beamed. "Thank you."

In fact, it was even better, because there was lots of American food in the supermarket that I had never even tried. But there was no supermarket selling Mum and my two little brothers; they could not be replaced or replicated, and I knew I could never leave them behind, not for good. I felt torn in two; split between two families and two countries. It was always hard leaving Manchester, seeing my brothers' tear-stained faces in the departure lounge. Yet it was equally hard leaving Mazen, my new husband, behind in Lebanon. When I was in Saida, Yousef and Maz would send me little notes or paint pictures for me, which I looked forward to. But if anything, it made me miss them even more.

"Home soon," I promised Yousef when we spoke on the phone.

"Back soon," I promised Mazen, as we hugged goodbye at the airport.

In the meantime, every spare penny we had went on our fight to be together. But to our dismay, our appeal was rejected, and we were advised to apply yet again.

"What more can we do?" I asked wearily.

But we were both determined never to give up. Our love was real, and eventually, the authorities would have to accept that.

6

In September 2008, soon after Yousef's seventh birthday, I discovered I was pregnant. I was over the moon. All through my teenage years, I'd loved being a second mummy, a little mother hen, to Yousef and then Maz and I enjoyed my job in the nursery too. I'd always longed for a baby of my own. It was bittersweet because of course Mazen was still stuck in Lebanon, still trying to get a visa. But I video-called him for every scan and check-up. And during the early part of the pregnancy, I managed one visit to Saida, so that Mazen could lay his head on my stomach and listen to the early sounds of our baby stirring in the womb.

"I love you so much," he told me.

"Me too," I replied.

The problem was, we had to convince the authorities of that too. We were both interviewed again, separately, at the embassy.

"Our relationship is real," I insisted. "We're in love, we're having a baby, we just want to be together as a family."

It was so frustrating. Mazen had enough money to support me and the baby; he wasn't asking for benefits or help of any sort. By now, he had finished his studies and he was working full time in an engineering firm. His family, still, generously contributed to flights and legal costs. But as time went on, his legal bills from the visa application spiralled, and the money that we could have spent on a home, and a cot, and a pram, was instead being wasted on endless visa appeals. The pregnancy was lonely without Mazen and I had complications too. I suffered from dehydration and sickness and was admitted to hospital with hyperemesis on and off for most of the pregnancy. It was so worrying, more so for Mazen because he couldn't be with me.

"I feel so helpless," he confessed.

In June 2009, my labour finally began, and Mum and I set off to the hospital. I was buzzing with anticipation, with Mazen on video-call the whole way there. But the contractions were stop-start and irregular, and after I was checked out, the midwives sent me home. The next night, the same thing happened. I was so anxious to meet my baby and of course Mazen was too. He was on a permanent video call that whole week.

"Don't worry," Mum reassured me. "The baby will come when he's ready."

On the third night, I woke with painful contractions in my lower back. This time, they were regular and coming more quickly. The baby was on his way, I was sure of it. It was around 2am and the house was quiet. I tiptoed into Mum's room, and whispered:

"I think it's definitely time."

To my surprise, she flung off the duvet and leapt out of bed – fully dressed!

"Best to be prepared!" she grinned and grabbed my hospital bag. Ghaleb was there to look after Yousef and Maz, and Mum took me to St Mary's Hospital. All the way there, Mazen was on video call, following my labour, sharing every moment.

Our little boy, Raafat, was born eleven hours later, perfectly healthy and weighing 6lbs 9ozs. It was a difficult birth and I needed lots of stitches, but the memory of the pain melted away like a snowflake when I held him for the first time. I felt my heart singing with love. Every bone of my body seemed to beam and glow with happiness. On the other end of the phone, Mazen was celebrating; dancing around his apartment and crying tears of pure joy. I wished so much he could be with me. But I knew I was blessed too, because I had Mum to take good care of me, and Yousef and little Maz idolised their new nephew. As they peered over his crib, eyes round with wonder, I had a flashback to myself, staring at Yousef when he was born, hardly able to believe my luck.

"Is he really ours?" they asked. "For keeps?"

At home, we settled into a contented routine. Yousef continued to make amazing progress. He began reading the Harry Potter series, and after those, the Percy Jackson books. After he finished each one, I'd pick pages at random and test him on various facts.

"What is Professor Sprout's first name?" I asked him.

"And what is the fourth book in the Percy Jackson series?"

Yousef was always ready with his answer, and it was almost impossible to catch him out. And yet, despite his gift for learning, Yousef was in many ways an ordinary little boy. He loved playing football with his pals, and for his birthday he got a Manchester United shirt with his name and a number 7 on the back, for his favourite player, Ronaldo. After school, and at weekends, he spent hours playing outside with his friends; football, basketball, or riding their bikes up and down our street. He and little Maz plotted against us with funny pranks, or they rolled around the living room play-fighting. They had a particular magic trick which they loved to perform, involving a vanishing coin underneath a glass. Maz wore a magician's cloak from a dressing-up set and Yousef held a plastic wand. Mum was in the audience, and I was in charge of film and lighting.

"Wow!" Mum gasped, when the coin mysteriously vanished. "That is amazing."

Another one of their favourite jokes was to spread chocolate sauce on a paper towel and leave it on the bathroom floor, and then wait for Mum to shriek, right on cue, the moment she walked into the bathroom.

"Who has been for a poo?" she demanded, playing the role perfectly, whilst Yousef and Maz crouched on the landing outside and laughed until they cried.

"She falls for it every time," Yousef said to me, as if he couldn't believe how gullible Mum was.

It was a funny little moment, a trick replicated probably in thousands of households with young children across the world. But that makes it perhaps all the more precious and poignant.

And alongside reading about The Spanish Armada or perhaps the digestive system, Yousef equally enjoyed flicking through *Match of the Day* magazine each week, or the Manchester United magazine every month. He was a collector too: stones, stamps, and football cards. He always had something in his pockets or grasped in his little hands. Like any other little boy, he might get a McDonald's as a treat on Saturdays. And in addition to watching documentaries, he and Maz also loved watching Fireman Sam and Disney cartoons. Yousef's favourite film was: 'Kangaroo Jack' where he knew the entire script.

By the time he turned ten years old, his teacher revealed, at parents' evening, that he was taking extra training in order to keep up with him.

"I don't want to hold him back, so I'm looking at ways to keep him challenged," he explained to us. "I even let him teach the class the other day, to explain how clouds are made.

"When he's finished his own work, he goes around the other tables, helping the other children. I've never come across a child like him.

"We've just finished a wall display about space, and Yousef produced an excellent piece of writing about a rocket. I'm going to keep it on the wall, because I truly believe that one day, he'll be famous."

Mum was very appreciative, but she was also humble, and keen to keep Yousef grounded. She taught him to be grateful to his teachers, for showing such faith in him, and to be thankful for the academic talents he had been given. Yousef was still in year 5 when the same teacher asked Mum to attend school for a meeting, and, as was always the way, I went along too.

"We really feel that Yousef ought to apply for a scholarship to grammar school," he told us. "It means doing an entrance exam, which he has to pass, but we will support him all we can."

Mum was not convinced at first. Everyone we knew, me and Rachel included, had attended the local high school. We had done perfectly well. Nobody from our community, as far as we knew, had ever been to grammar school.

"How would we afford it?" Mum worried. "How would he even get there? What if it doesn't fit in and he hates it? What if he does fit in and he hates us?"

She thought it over, and spoke to Yousef, who was predictably brimming with enthusiasm, and impatient to sit the exams. He couldn't see any drawbacks at all.

"I have to give him a chance," Mum decided. "He can sit the exams, and who knows, he might pass one, he might not. We can make a plan after that."

In the Autumn of year 6, his final year of primary school, Yousef sat the exams for half a dozen grammar schools, all dotted around the Greater Manchester area. We'd heard that most children required extra tuition in the run-up to the exams, arranged privately, but naturally Mum couldn't afford anything like that. We just left Yousef to his own devices and hoped for the best. We didn't even know exactly what the exams entailed. But the upside of that was of course that Yousef was under no pressure whatsoever. For the exams, he and Mum took the bus to each grammar school in turn; Mum loved having a little nosy around each elite school, taking in the entrance halls, the posh carpets, the manicured lawns.

"You should have seen it, Jade," she'd tell me. "The soap in the toilets was lovely."

It became something of a jolly day out; Mum packing sandwiches each morning and Yousef wheedling a McDonald's out of her instead on the way home! The focus was on the fast-food treat afterwards, and not on the exam itself. I didn't notice it really at the time, but it was Mum's way of deflecting the stress away from the exam and it worked perfectly. She was so clever and yet so subtle. In the following weeks, as we waited for the results, Yousef grinned and said to Mum:

"If I pass, will you hire a limo to take me and my friends for a ride on the last day of school?"

Mum nodded, distractedly.

"Let's see if you pass first," she replied.

When the first letter dropped through the door, Yousef ran to open it. He had no nerves at all, no thought whatsoever of failure. After all, he had nothing to lose.

"I did it!" he yelled. "They've offered me a place!"

Mum and I looked at each other and burst into surprised laughter.

"You'd better get that limo booked," I chuckled.

Over the next few days, Yousef got replies from all the other schools and incredibly, he had been accepted at every single one. Not only that, but he had smashed the exams too, scoring an average 98 per cent. Now, instead of the schools choosing him, Yousef was choosing the school!

"You can go anywhere you fancy," I beamed.

Immediately, he picked Manchester Grammar School, MGS. It was the best school on the list, the most prestigious, the most famous. Alumni included Oscar-winning actor Ben Kingsley, Nobel-prize winning chemist John Polanyi and England cricket captain Michael Atherton, along with a long list of respected writers, historians, and musicians; many of whom had gone on to become knights of the realm. But, equally important in Yousef's eyes, it was on our bus route! On the number 50 bus, it was just four stops away.

"At least I won't have to get up too early," he said to me.

True to her word, Mum scraped together enough to pay for a limousine to pick Yousef and his mates up on the last day of term at primary school and drive them back to our house for a celebration. As the party drew to a close, Mum and I sat chatting in the kitchen, surrounded by the usual party debris of half-eaten fairy cakes and paper cups filled with warm lemonade, whilst Yousef and his friends played football in the back garden.

"This is the start of a new life for him," Mum said dreamily. "This is his way out."

7

The MGS brochure arrived in the weeks after, and Yousef thumbed through it quickly, enthralled by each new detail.

"Look!" he pointed, showing me the photographs. "Football pitches like Wembley, cricket pitches like Lord's, tennis courts like Wimbledon! I can't wait."

There was more good news too, in June of that same year. After five appeals and a staggering £30,000 on legal fees, Mazen was finally granted permission to come and live in the UK. Our solicitor called with the news, and I burst into tears, a mixture of disbelief and sheer relief.

"Are you sure?" I asked him, over and over. "Are you absolutely sure?"

After all this time, after so much heartache, expense and stress, it just didn't seem real. By now, Raafat was three years old. He had spent his early years back and forth from Lebanon, visiting his daddy, and he actually believed that Mazen lived in the airport. He had no idea that we were all supposed to be living in the same house together. Thanks to the authorities, his perception of family life was completely skewed.

"We're all going to live together," I told Raafat. "You, me and Daddy!"

Two weeks on, Mazen landed at Manchester Airport, and I sank into his arms.

"Welcome home," I beamed. "This is where you belong."

Mazen could not wait to ride in a black cab; for him, they were quintessentially British, and number one on his tourist bucket list.

"We'd better get the bus home," I laughed. "We've spent quite enough on travel for now!"

Outside the house, Yousef and Maz were waiting with home-made 'Welcome Mazen' signs and inside, Mum had organised a little party and all our friends and neighbours came to welcome him. Soon after, we moved into our own flat nearby, and Mazen settled in well in Manchester. Yet for months he felt the cold badly and even on a warm summer's day, he would wrap up in a fleece and scarf.

"When's the sun coming out?" he asked.

"Never," I laughed.

That summer was so busy; alongside Mazen's arrival we were preparing for Yousef to move to grammar school too. He had won a full scholarship for the £12,000 a year fees, and Mum was awarded a 50 per cent reduction on all expenses. She also found a second-hand swap-shop, where parents of less fortunate pupils could pick up uniforms, sports kits, and pieces of equipment. Even so, it was a huge strain financially; paying 50 per cent was still a big ask for her. By now, she was unable to work full-time, due to her arthritis, and her condition was very unpredictable. She took around thirty different tablets daily and was often at the doctors. Yousef took a real interest in her condition; he read up on arthritis and was forever suggesting ways she could try to ease the pain. He knew every tablet that she took, every dosage.

"When I'm older I'll find a cure for arthritis," he promised her. "I'll make you better."

"I've every faith in you," Mum replied.

She did her best to hold down a part-time nursing job, but sometimes she was literally crippled with pain, and she couldn't even leave the house. It was around that time too that she and Ghaleb separated for good. They had been on and off for so many years, arguing over money – or the lack of it – and both with very different opinions too – and though they had tried to keep the family together, it wasn't to be. So now, Mum would have to manage as a single mum, battling a disability also. Funding Yousef at MGS was a big worry certainly, but it was outweighed by our pride at his achievements. And of course at this stage, we were blissfully ignorant, with no real idea of what to expect at a grammar school.

For Yousef's first day, in September 2013, we were all up for 6am, humming with nervous energy. Mum had splashed out and hired a minibus taxi so that we could all go along to wave him off.

"We're like The Waltons," Mum giggled, as I loaded Raafat's pram into the taxi, and Mazen and Maz climbed in after me. Yousef rolled his eyes, doing his best to appear embarrassed, but he was grinning widely. And he looked so smart too, in his blue shirt, his navy blazer, and his tie. As we pulled up outside the school, there was a collective intake of breath inside the taxi.

"This place is like Hogwarts," Maz whistled.

The school itself was imposing; austere, commanding, and with rows and rows of slightly disapproving windows. The buildings sat majestically in extensive grounds, with sports pitches and courts as far as I could see. It was mind-blowing. We were just four bus stops – but a whole world away – from the council estate that we called home. I struggled to grasp that my little brother was actually going to attend this school. And equally jaw-dropping were the other arrivals, now clustering around us.

"Look," Mum nudged me.

Just next to our taxi, a Rolls Royce purred to a halt, and a chauffeur got out. I squealed, thinking that maybe there was a celebrity arriving. Instead, he opened the back door and out jumped a young boy, wearing the same uniform as Yousef. On our other side, there were pupils arriving in Bentleys, Ferraris and Porsches. Some were chauffeur driven, others were accompanied by nannies. I thought of how Mum had scrimped to afford the £8 cost of our minibus taxi; it had seemed like such an extravagance, but she had justified it by the magnitude of the occasion. Now, her splurge seemed paltry. She and I exchanged stunned looks and there was something else too, between us. An expanding panic. Had we made a big mistake? Yousef was already skipping off up the wide driveway.

"Come on!" he called.

We were taken into the big entrance hall, and I felt as though I was entering another universe completely. I might just as well have climbed through a wardrobe, straight into

Narnia. The hall was cold and unfriendly, with lofty ceilings and wooden panelling. I felt completely out of my depth, but I was determined not to show it, though I imagine, looking back, that just made it all the more obvious. Yousef went to sit on the stage with all the other new boys; his face was a picture; bright-eyed and raring to go. He was itching to get started. Whilst the head of year gave an induction speech, Yousef risked a cheeky little wave in my direction, and I felt a warmth inside. I felt instantly better. He was so at ease here; unlike me. He had a confidence and a self-assuredness I would never have, and I knew he would need it in buckets full at a school like this. After the speeches, Yousef filed out with his new classmates, down a corridor, and I watched and smiled until he was almost out of sight. Inexplicably, as his dark head disappeared into the throng, I felt a conflicting stab of sadness. This was a happy day, a proud day. But there was an undercurrent too of fear that we might lose him here, anxiety that he might be swallowed up and spat back out, by this wealth and privilege and prestige.

"Stay true to yourself, Yousef," I whispered.

Mum was quiet and pensive as we walked out, into the sunshine, and I fancied she was thinking the same. For the journey home, we caught the bus; we couldn't afford a taxi both ways. As we waited at the bus stop, with Raafat crying in the pram and Maz grumbling that he was starving, the chauffeurs and the posh cars rolled past us, blinkered and unseeing. It hit me that the gulf between the two worlds was much wider and deeper than any of us had anticipated.

8

Yousef seemed to settle in well at MGS and any doubts I had about him not slotting in gradually dissipated. He came home each day bursting with new facts and information.

"So," he'd say. "If you just multiply it by itself, you end up with the number 7, every time. Think about it."

"Yousef, it's way above my head," I confessed. "Tell me again, more slowly."

I'd done well in my own GCSEs and I'd left education with a diploma in child-care and child psychology, but I was no match for Yousef. In fact, nobody was. We started calling him: 'Professor Yousef' and of course he loved that. As the weeks passed, he expressed surprise – and some relief – that the other boys in his classes weren't as outlandishly clever as he'd feared.

"Some of the kids in my class have private tutors for every subject," he told me. "And they're still struggling in school. The work really isn't as difficult as I'd expected. I'm doing well so far. I can hold my own no problem."

We were pleased. But if Yousef wasn't struggling, Mum was. He tried out for the rugby team and was successful, so he needed a rugby kit. He read out a seemingly endless list of requirements.

"Socks, shorts, short-sleeved and long-sleeved shirts, base layer, mouthguard, helmet, boots."

Then, he needed a football kit. The cost of these extras was at least three times higher at MGS than at state schools. Even with the assistance that came from Yousef's bursary status, Mum found it a strain.

"The rugby and football kits literally cost hundreds," she told me.

But she was always so careful not to let Yousef and Maz see that she was having difficulties. She tried to give Yousef everything he needed, no matter what it took.

"The boys come first," she said. "It was always the same with you and Rachel when you were small."

I understood completely. Now a mum myself, I shared her sentiments. Raafat was three and a half years old and ever since his arrival we had been keen to add to our family, hampered of course by Mazen being stuck in Lebanon for much of that time. I had suffered two early miscarriages, in 2010 and 2011, and then in 2012, I'd fallen pregnant again. Despite extreme sickness, just as with Raafat, I got past the all-important 12-week milestone, and I began to look forward to our new arrival. But in January 2013, at 26 weeks, our son, Adam, had been stillborn. The loss was harrowing; I felt swamped by grief. It felt as though everyone around me was having babies and adding to their families. Everyone except me.

"I had got so far into the pregnancy," I sobbed. "I really thought he might make it."

But we became all the more determined to try again; we wanted so much to have another child. The doctors could find no obvious explanation as to why I had carried Raafat full term, but yet none of the other babies had made it. Mum was increasingly worried about the physical and emotional impact on me too. By now, I'd been pregnant four times and had only one living child.

"Maybe it's not meant to be, love," she said. "You have Raafat, and he's a little miracle."

She was right; we all doted on Raafat. And in addition to looking after my little boy, I took on the role of Mum's carer, because her arthritis was getting worse. Each morning, when her joints were stiff, I went back to the family home, to help with breakfast and the school run. After school, I'd return to Mum's and in the evenings, Mazen would come there, straight from work, and we'd all eat together. We were one big family, and I loved that feeling of cohesion and togetherness. I drew strength from it.

But more than once, as she prepared meals, I noticed that Mum was nibbling on a bowl of cereal, whilst serving grilled chicken or a stew for the rest of the family.

"I'm not hungry," she protested. "I prefer cereal, really I do."

At first, I thought that perhaps her arthritis was affecting her appetite. I knew she took heavy duty medication which maybe was making her nauseous. But over the next few months, I realised that she was simply trying to save money. She prioritised the healthy food for the boys and left herself out. That was typical of Mum; she put everyone else before herself, time after time. And yet even when I confronted her, she wouldn't admit it.

"I would much rather have cereal," she insisted. "That's the truth."

In the evenings, when Mazen and I were taking the children home, Yousef would always sprint along the pavement, trying to outrun our car, and making the little ones laugh.

"He never runs out of energy," I said, in wonder. "It's as though he has a reserve tank somewhere."

It was perhaps in January 2014, at the start of his second term at MGS, when I voiced my surprise that I hadn't met any of Yousef's new friends yet.

"Me neither," Mum said. "I don't understand it. I've asked him more than once to invite some of his new pals round, but he won't. He goes to their houses sometimes after school, but he doesn't ask them back here.

"I can't work it out. He's normally so sociable."

Yousef at first clammed up, insisting nothing was wrong. But the niggle ate away at me. And we noticed other little changes in him too. As northerners, we had always eaten a traditional breakfast, dinner, and tea. But now Yousef insisted we changed the names to breakfast, lunch, and dinner. At first, we just thought it was a quirk; he was subject to so many new influences at MGS and, like a leaf in the wind, he was being buffeted about from one viewpoint to the next. It was completely understandable.

"I don't mind what you call it," Mum said. "As long as you wash the dishes afterwards!"

Yousef would normally have a witty come-back ready, but he just scowled and slunk off to his room, which was not like him.

Then one day, Mum was preparing a snack, and asked him:

"Do you want cheese on your butty?"

Yousef frowned with visible distaste.

"Don't say butty, say sandwich," he corrected her.

Mum smiled, but she was crestfallen; I could tell.

"Don't be such a snob, Yousef," I interjected. "There's nothing wrong with the way Mum speaks. We've always said butty, you know that."

It felt as though he was picking holes in his own life, his own background. But I knew that the criticism must have come first-hand from some of his new pals at school and I realised this was the cause of his recent moodiness.

"We've still never met your new friends," I reminded him. "Why don't you ever invite them round?"

Yousef mumbled another half-baked excuse. But he couldn't side-step the issue forever. At primary school, his mates had been round at our house most evenings and Mum was forever throwing in another chicken leg for tea or making up a bed on the sofa for an extra guest. But now, for Yousef, that all stopped. Eventually, he snapped:

"I don't like being a bursary boy. That's what they call me: 'Bursary Boy'! It's so embarrassing. I don't want to be different. I want to be like all my mates at school. And I don't want to live in a council house either. Why should we have to live round here, when some of my mates live in palaces? It's just not fair and I'm sick of it."

The disappointment spread right across Mum's face and seemed to seep down, through her sagging shoulders, as she slumped onto a chair. My heart went out to her, and I turned on Yousef, my temper rising.

"You're the one who's not being fair," I said sharply to him. "You should be proud of your family, and where you come from. Never be ashamed of who you are. Mum makes a lot of sacrifices for you to go to that school and you know it."

Yousef sighed sulkily.

"I'm not bringing anyone round here," he pouted. "The kids at my school arrive in Bentleys and Maseratis. One boy actually has a helicopter. We don't even have a car! Mum doesn't even drive any more!"

I thought back to our battered minibus taxi, on Yousef's first day at school. It was fast becoming a metaphor for the chasm which existed between Yousef and his rich friends. It was understandable, I supposed. Inevitable even. Yousef was an impressionable and naive 12-year-old, and it was probably, definitely, asking too much for him not to be seduced by the glamorous lifestyles of his new pals and the glossy and impermanent veneer of money. He was now seeing his home and his hand-to-mouth existence through the prism of extreme privilege and finding it sadly lacking. Yet though our home and our lifestyle was very humble, the architecture of our family, of the people in it, was strong and solid. I didn't know how to convey that to Yousef; it was a lesson I hoped he wouldn't learn the hard way.

"All that glitters is not gold," Mum told him softly. "You should know that quote, Yousef. It's Shakespeare."

But once again, he stomped off to his bedroom and he slammed the door.

"He's at that age," I sighed, slipping an arm around Mum's shoulder. "It's all hormones. Just ignore him."

But the fact that Yousef could outshine his new class-mates academically hadn't helped either; it had simply made him more arrogant and superior. Now that he was amongst these elite students, and he saw they were no brighter or better than he was, he felt entitled, he felt aggrieved, and he wanted what they had. From my experience, as a little girl in Texas and now with Yousef at grammar school, money soured everything. I just didn't see the big appeal of wealth at all. Yet the comparisons continued. Over the February half-term, his friends jetted off to Dubai or to the Caribbean. He had one friend who was going to the Maldives. Others had their own ski lodges in Switzerland, Austria and France.

"Where are we going in half-term?" Yousef demanded. "What have you booked for us?"

"Nando's, if you're lucky," Mum retorted, and she and I stifled a giggle.

Most of the time we managed Yousef's childish sulks with humour. He was just being a stroppy teenager after all; it was simply another phase of his development. Those months were a learning process, and not just for him. I quickly realised that though he was academically gifted, he was also, like any other prepubescent boy, maddeningly immature, woefully self-absorbed, and locked in his own selfish little bubble. It was just a part of growing up. His education at home – his acceptance of who he was, and who others were – was every bit as important as what he learned behind the hallowed walls of MGS. And Mum and I made it our job to keep his feet firmly on the ground, though at times it felt as though we might need to cement them in place.

"One of my mates gets £200 a week, just to spend on stuff," Yousef told us.

"And another one came to school in a Lamborghini this week."

"And he has his own swimming pool, in a basement in his house."

Mum winked at me over Yousef's head.

"Why would you need a swimming pool, when we've got a perfectly good bath upstairs? I can't even get you to shower every day, never mind about taking a swim!"

Yousef flounced off in a mood and Mum's smile faded. Sometimes, it was hard for her to stay buoyant, especially when her health was bad, in those damp winter months. In truth, though she never admitted it to Yousef, there were many times when she bitterly regretted sending him to grammar school. Yes, he was getting a marvellous education and there were untold opportunities and connections to be had in the rarefied environment at MGS. But the school, or rather the pupils there, had thrown up a whole host of other challenges.

"I thought going to a school like that would make him into a better person," she told me, with an air of flat resignation. "Instead, he's turning into someone we hardly know. I feel like I'm losing him sometimes, Jade. I feel like we're not good enough for him anymore."

It was a horrible, gut-wrenching thought. But Yousef was a boy trapped, suspended, between two worlds. And in the event, he belonged in neither.

9

In the spring term, the annual Activities Week came around, where the pupils could choose between a range of pursuits and sports; football, rugby, water polo, trekking and mountain biking. The vast majority of families probably didn't give the costs a second thought, but Mum had to plan ahead, and budget, so that Yousef could take part. Privately, we both hoped that he would choose one of the less extravagant pursuits. But equally, we knew we could never have influenced him to do so. Despite her reservations and her regrets, Mum was adamant that she would keep up with the expenses. Somehow.

Mazen promised to speak to Yousef about his behaviour and his priorities and I had high hopes that he would be able to make him see sense. Mazen was quietly spoken but principled and firm, and he had a good rapport with Yousef. They shared a close bond.

"I'll do my best with him," Mazen assured me.

By now, Mum had to make a decision about Maz's secondary education too. Maz was also very bright, but he was much more reticent than Yousef and less self-assured.

"I really don't think MGS is the school for Maz," Mum told me. "I worry about how he might cope."

She discussed it with Maz, who instead opted to go to the local high school, with all of his friends.

"You will do really well," I said to him. "And you'll be at home there too."

During that first summer holidays, Yousef saw more of his old pals; he played out in the street, he rode his bike around the estate, and he settled back into the routine he'd had at primary school. Many of his new friends were away for the summer too, so he had less contact with them. It was just like the old days, and it was like having little Yo-Yo back again.

"You obviously got through to him," I said to Mazen. "Mum is so pleased."

She and I were secretly thrilled. The super-cars and the helicopter pads and the designer clothes seemed a world away. Yousef was perfectly happy with a weekend in Blackpool and a trip to the Trafford Centre. They were simple pleasures, but we had so much fun. And I held the memories of those days close to my heart.

10

Year 8 came, and Yousef continued to do well at school. But once he was settled into the school routine, he continued once more to envy the extravagant lifestyles enjoyed by his peers. Mum and I, and in particular, Mazen, did our best to keep him in touch with reality. Our reality.

"Having a Porsche doesn't make you a better person," Mazen told him. "You are rich in other ways, Yousef. Look at your loving family. Look at your talents. You have so much to be grateful for."

And, after he turned 14, Yousef slowly started to show small but perceptible signs of thinking for himself. One evening, when Mum was cooking his tea as usual, he sauntered into the kitchen and said:

"You know, some of my mates have chefs or nannies to cook for them. Not many have a mum around like you are. I'm glad I've got you."

Mum beamed.

"I'm glad I've got you, too," she said.

And on another occasion, when Raafat was jumping all over him on the sofa, he said to me:

"My mates are so envious of my little nephew, and the way we all get on and we see each other every day. I've shown them photos of Raafat, and they think he's cute. It's cool being an uncle."

Now, it was my turn to beam, not only at the praise for my sons but at the fact that Yousef was making progress, emotionally and socially. And as the weeks spun into months, instead of hiding the fact that he was on a bursary, he learned to be proud of it. His entire viewpoint changed and flipped and with it, he slowly began to appreciate us all, especially Mum.

"I spent ages being jealous of my mates and now they're actually jealous of me!" he told us. "They think I'm lucky to have Mum and all of you around all the time. One of my mate's parents both live abroad, and he hardly sees them. He just has staff in the house!"

I almost choked on my coffee.

"You're kidding!" I spluttered.

Now that he was growing up and maturing a little, Yousef at last began inviting his friends round to the house to meet us.

"I'm in such a panic," Mum confessed. "It's been such a big build-up that now he's actually got mates coming round, I don't know what to cook, or what to do. I've cleaned the entire house."

"Mum, they're just kids," I consoled her. "Don't worry. Kids, but a bit different."

And it was true, some of his friends were innately and irreversibly different. The way they carried themselves, the type of clothes they wore, the confidence and nonchalance with which they sailed through life; it was all alien to us. It was as though they were members of an exclusive club, and we could never have passed the entrance exam, because we didn't know the questions, never mind the answers. No amount of qualifications, or cash, would ever change that. But these were mere trappings, and beyond the differences, there were many more similarities. These were just regular boys, after all, like Yousef and Maz, who, it turned out, loved Mum's cooking, and the infectious chaos and warmth of her home. They laughed when she danced around the kitchen with her music blaring. They held up their plates eagerly when she offered second helpings. They were kind and patient with Raafat. I realised that we had no more right to judge them than they did us. It was wonderful, during those visits, to see Yousef settle into an easy equilibrium, which suited both his school and home life. He was finally happy in his own skin, and given the challenges and influences he was facing, that seemed like no small achievement. He made one friend in particular too, Yas, who, like him, was from a working-class background, without especial wealth or privilege. Yas was a lovely kid, and the two of them became good friends.

"Not everyone is different to me," Yousef conceded. "I can see that now."

Early in year 9, Yousef arrived home from school excitedly waving a letter in his hand.

"China!" he announced. "There's a school trip to China! Can I go? Please? I promise I won't ask for anything else! Please?"

Mum smiled at his eagerness, but I saw clouds of panic scudding across her face too. Later, I glanced at the letter on the kitchen table and gasped.

"Three grand!"

"I know," Mum replied, her shoulders cowed with the sheer weight of the worry. "I know. Where am I going to find that sort of money?"

But despite the enormity of the challenge there was never any question – none at all – that Yousef wouldn't be allowed to go. He was studying Chinese and doing really well too. There was no way Mum would have denied him a place on a trip of a lifetime.

"Mazen and I will chip in, Mum," I promised. "You know that."

But even so, we didn't have much money either. Mazen worked hard in the chemist, and I spent my time looking after Raafat and caring for Mum. Mazen and I were still trying for another baby, but to date I had suffered six miscarriages, each early in the pregnancy, each another agonising loss. The grief became worse, not easier, after each one. But nonetheless, I refused to give up on my dream. I was all about family, and I wanted to try everything I could to give Raafat a little brother or sister. In the meantime, I wanted to help Mum out with my own little brothers, and I gave her what I could, each week, towards the China holiday. She arranged with school to pay the trip off in instalments, and in the months beforehand, she made savings wherever she could. I noticed her nibbling on cereal or toast most evenings, instead of sitting down for the evening meal.

"I prefer toast," she told me again. "I'm not keen on chicken."

She took out a loan too, and every Wednesday a man named Paul came to the door to collect her weekly payment. I knew she was probably paying back double in interest, but I also knew she had too much pride and dignity to complain about it. It turned out that Paul was a nice bloke and if it was raining, he'd often come in and have a cup of tea and a natter with Mum. That was so typical of her; she'd see the best of any situation, and make friends with anyone, even the loan man! By the time the trip came around she had somehow paid off the whole amount, with spending money too.

As with Yousef's first day at high school, we hired a minibus taxi to Manchester Airport, in October 2015, to wave him off. It was a ten-day holiday, with two of those days staying with a Chinese family. He wasn't allowed to take a mobile phone, but the school sent regular updates, and each night we all crowded around the laptop to see the latest photos and news.

"I miss him so much," Mum smiled, her eyes shiny with tears. "I know it's only ten days, but it feels like such a long time."

We couldn't help thinking back too, to his first trip abroad without us, when he'd had to be air-lifted home from the war in Lebanon. We both hoped there would be no similar drama this time. But at the end of the ten days, Yousef landed back in Manchester safe and sound, and the trip had been a resounding success. He had learned so much; widened his horizons and stretched his imagination right out. He had bought me a little Chinese flag, as a keepsake.

"This is exactly what I wanted for him at MGS," Mum grinned. "I want his world to be bigger than mine. I want him to feel that nothing is impossible."

And after China, Yousef seemed to have grown up a little more. Weeks later, there was a school trip to France, but Yousef didn't even bring the letter home. We only heard about the holiday through one of his pals.

"Didn't you fancy it?" I asked him.

"Nah," he replied. "I went to China, that was enough. Mum should be spending her money on something else."

I threw my arms around him; empathy was a difficult concept for all teenage boys, but it seemed like Yousef was finally getting the message. When the annual Activities Week came around again, Yousef chose the cheapest options on the list, without any prompting. He still pestered Mum for the latest trainers or a designer T-shirt, as any teenage boy might, but it was always more in hope than expectation. He knew he had to save up for a treat, week by week, just like the rest of us. But long after the trip to China was nothing more than a distant memory, Mum was still paying the loan man every Wednesday. And it was too tempting, as time went on, to add another £50 for school shoes, £150 for washing machine repairs, £70 for birthday presents.

"There's always something," she told me, shaking her head. "Always another bill to pay."

That loan became a long-standing fixture in our lives, and one, a little like a virus, that we just couldn't seem to shake.

11

As well as spending lots of time with Yas, Yousef had brought home another boy too, Adam Chowdhary, who was in that same group of friends at MGS.

Adam was one of the very wealthy boys, his family were reportedly millionaires, and he lived in an affluent area of Cheshire. Mum was impressed when she met Adam; he had hopes of becoming a dentist, and he was extremely well-mannered and polite.

"I think he will be a good influence on Yousef, and Yousef on him too," she told me. "They're very different boys, but they seem to get on well together."

One of the reasons she had been in favour of sending Yousef to MGS was to mix with children who had been raised in nicer areas, with lower crime rates, fewer stabbings, shootings, and murders. There was a great sense of community where we lived, and we loved our estate, but it was blighted by crime. Mum wanted better for Yousef, she wanted a brighter future for him, and she saw MGS, and the friends he made there, as his ticket out.

However, even though some of Yousef's friends were from extreme wealth and privilege, Mum exercised the same strict vetting process over them as she always had with all of our friends. Yousef was not allowed to visit friends' houses until Mum had met their parents or at least spoken with them on the phone.

"Aww, Mum, really?" Yousef asked, recoiling with embarrassment.

"Yes, really," she said. "I need to know where you are and who you're spending time with. Money makes no difference to me."

I remembered being similarly mortified when she checked out my friends when I was younger. But now that I was a mother myself, I understood her sentiment perfectly and approved.

"Luckily for you, the calls went well, and you're allowed to sleep over at Adam's," she told Yousef with a smile.

Like all teenagers, Yousef was spreading his wings. But Mum, Mazen and I made sure his roots were firmly anchored. He had never been in any trouble with the school, not even a detention, and of course there had never been anything more serious either. He was a studious and hard-working boy, serious about his studies and his ambitions. He and Maz were expected to contribute at home; Mum had a list of household tasks underneath a magnet on the fridge. As little boys, they'd been so keen to help out, squabbling amongst themselves to take the responsibility for washing the dishes or collecting the dirty laundry from the bedrooms. But now, Yousef did all he could to bribe Maz or, more easily, Raafat into doing the chores on his behalf.

"They like helping me," Yousef insisted, with a cheeky smile. "We have good banter."

He was terminally lazy, but then, that wasn't unusual for a boy of his age. Mum's main complaint was that she didn't like Yousef's rap music blasting out of his bedroom.

"It's dreadful, no tune, no chorus," she told me. "And he swears a lot when he's playing FIFA too. I don't like bad language, never have done."

"I don't swear, as in actually swear," Yousef protested. "It's just banter, Mum. Honestly."

It was like a verbal tic; he would just plead 'banter' to everything and he was automatically absolved. One of his favourite songs was Drake's 'God's Plan' and he loved singing the lyrics to Mum:

'She said: "Do you love me?" I tell her, "Only partly."
I only love my bed and my momma, I'm sorry.'

The words could have been written just for him. All discipline forgotten; Mum found herself laughing. Yousef had that way about him; his own smile was so infectious that I would feel the corners of my mouth turning upwards, in spite of him and because of him. He had a smile to melt the hardest of hearts.

12

In the autumn of 2016 I fell pregnant for a tenth time. Mazen and I braced ourselves for disappointment, knowing that more than likely I would miscarry.

"Let's not tell anyone," I suggested. "At least until after we get to 12 weeks."

But the moment I saw Mum, she looked me up and down, and said shrewdly:

"Jade you have the 'tired eyes', I know you're pregnant."

I couldn't help but laugh. Mum could always guess when I was pregnant, because I had what she called 'tired eyes'. She had a sixth sense about these things, and it was a standing joke between us.

"You're right," I admitted. "I've done a test. But I'm keeping it quiet."

She was worried about me, I knew. Mazen and I had been through so much heartache with the loss of our babies. I was very sick during the pregnancy with hyperemesis, and, as before, I had to be hospitalised. I felt so rotten that I was sure the baby must be feeling it too. Each day, I expected to wake up, with the first signs of miscarriage. But amazingly, the weeks went on, and as we passed each milestone; 12 weeks, 20 weeks, 24 weeks, we began to dare to hope. Even so, I refused to buy a single piece of baby equipment; we had no pram, cot, or baby-clothes. After my 20-week scan, we threw a small gender reveal party, just for our family. Raafat was given the all-important task of cutting into the cake – and it showed a bright blue sponge inside.

"A boy! A boy!" he whooped. "This is what I wanted!"

I laughed. He reminded me so much of myself after I discovered that Mum was expecting a boy, all those years earlier, when she was pregnant with Yousef. But even towards the end of the pregnancy, I still harboured niggling doubts that something would go wrong. Mazen bought a pram the week before our baby was due, but I refused to tempt fate by having it in the house.

"Just in case," I said to him. "Let's keep it in the boot of the car."

Our son, Zack, was born in May 2017, by planned caesarean section. The moment I heard him cry, I knew that our agony was over. My rainbow baby was here at last. Lying in the hospital bed, with Zak's warm little body laid on my chest, I felt on top of the world; I was riding high on a tsunami of love and joy. The loss and heartache of the past few years was all washed away in that moment. Despite the surgery, I felt refreshed and cleansed; as though I was starting anew.

Zack weighed a little over 6lbs 5ozs. He had lots of dark hair and looked just like his uncles, and his big brother too. We all doted on him. We moved in with Mum for a while so that she could help out, after Mazen returned to work. But I made a good recovery from my surgery and devoted each day to enjoying my little boy. We had waited so long for him, and it just made me appreciate him all the more. Every smelly nappy, every late feed, every sleepless night, was a blessing and a privilege.

Around six weeks after the birth, I was enjoying a coffee with a friend, and she confided that she was plucking up courage to do a pregnancy test. She'd been trying for a baby for some time.

"I dread doing the tests each month, because I know it's going to be negative," she told me.

"Tell you what, let's get a double pack and I'll do a test too," I told her. "Make it fun. Mine will definitely be negative!"

We disappeared off into the loo and shortly afterwards we both emerged, completely white-faced.

"Mine was negative," she said.

"Mine was positive," I gasped.

I couldn't believe it. I'd only just given birth and now I was pregnant again! Fortunately the shock of my pregnancy was a distraction from my friend's negative test too. I called Mazen, at work, and he was overjoyed. He'd always wanted a big family. Next, I took the bus to Mum's house.

"You have the tired eyes," she said, as she opened the door, and we both started to laugh.

"You're like a psychic!" I replied. "I don't know how you do it!"

Though I was pleased, I was a little worried about how I'd cope with two babies so close in age together. Yet as it was, I was so busy looking after Raafat and Zack, and caring for Mum, that the weeks just whizzed by. I didn't even have time to get stressed. The pregnancy went well, without sickness or complications. This time, we decided to keep the gender a surprise, until the birth. Having carried two babies full term, I felt more confident and relaxed as the birth drew closer. Baby Daniel, our third son, was born in April 2018, again by caesarean section, and weighing 7lbs, so a little bigger than his brothers. He looked just like them and was certainly just as cute.

"All my mates are so jealous of me," Yousef said, as he enjoyed his first cuddle. "Three nephews! I'm so lucky."

After the heartache of our lost babies, the births of the boys felt nothing less than miraculous. The doctors couldn't say why, after all my miscarriages and the stillbirth, I'd been able to carry these two babies full term. I had once even been to a clinic in Coventry for testing but no reason for the miscarriages was ever found. Yousef did his own research; a fledgling little doctor even at his age! He'd send me various articles on what food to avoid and what supplements to take. I did everything I could. But in the end, we don't know what made the difference. It just felt as though Zack and Daniel were meant to be. With two babies, I had my hands full, of course, but Yousef and Maz were always around to help out. I filmed countless little clips of Yousef teaching Raafat how to box or how to play 'When the Reds go marching in' on the ukulele. Or he'd be bouncing the babies on his knee and sneaking secret chocolate buttons for Zack.

"These will be lovely memories for you all when you're grown up," I said, as I finished filming a keepy-up contest in the garden, with Yousef losing on purpose, Raafat running around in celebration, and Zack toddling after him, whooping without really knowing why. "We'll look back on these clips when you're all old and grey and we'll smile."

Never for a moment did I think that my tall, handsome brother, strong, reliable and seemingly indestructible, would not be given the chance to grow up. Never for a moment did I think he would be scythed down before his adult adventure even began.

Yousef's GCSE exams were due to start the month after Daniel was born. As they drew nearer, we began encouraging him to study and revise but for the most part, he was maddeningly laid-back and relaxed.

"It's too soon yet," he insisted. "If I revise now, I'll forget everything."

His best subjects were the sciences and he still had ambitions to become a doctor, maybe even a surgeon. From being a little boy, he'd shown such a keen interest in science and medicine. I thought back to him reading Mum's medical books, and it seemed like a natural progression for him to make this his career, if he could. Medicine, we knew, was highly competitive but we also knew that Yousef was highly capable. His weakest subjects were probably languages and music, yet even so he could speak Chinese and he could play the guitar and ukulele.

By now, he was growing into a typical 16-year-old; his bedroom was a mess of sweaty clothes, various cans of pungent deodorant, and half-eaten bowls of cereal. The wastepaper bin was stuffed with empty crisp packets, Coke cans and balls of screwed up paper. On his walls there were footballer stickers and Manchester Utd posters; reminders of a little boy from not so long ago. His room, or rather the deplorable state it was in, was a constant source of frustration for Mum.

"I have to wait until he goes out before I can blitz the place," she told me. "I keep the windows open whilst he's at school and then I Febreze everything he owns. I've even Febrezed him when he's been asleep, and he doesn't even sneeze!"

One evening, as they ate together, I overheard Yousef asking Mazen to teach him how to shave, and I giggled to myself. It was lovely, the way he confided in Mazen.

"You need a decent razor, I'll get you one, same as mine," Mazen told him. "Leave it with me."

But then he laughed and added:

"Yousef, it's a five-minute walk in between each hair on your chin. You need tweezers, not a razor!"

"Not true!" Yousef yelled. "I've got great designer stubble. I've got lots of girls after me. I have!"

Mum and I were laughing now too. Yousef was probably keen to start shaving because of what it signified, not because he needed to. But there was no denying that he was growing up and shaving his chin fluff was another step on the road to adulthood.

He was becoming very lazy in the mornings too, sleeping later and later, and it was an achievement just to get him out of bed and onto the bus. It was one of my jobs, and easily the most testing one, when I arrived at Mum's in the mornings, to get Yousef up before 7.30am.

"Yousef!" I shouted. "Wake up! I've got a jug of cold water and I'll pour it right down your ear if you don't move!"

"Yousef! I've called school. MGS are sending a truancy officer round now!"

"Yousef! Raafat and Zack are trying on your favourite Armani T-shirt!"

But nothing roused him. He always dragged himself out of bed at the last possible moment, skipping breakfast, tearing the house apart for a missing protractor or a PE shirt, and dashing out of the door with a cereal bar, in a higgledy-piggledy hurry.

"Bye!" he'd yell, "Love you!" and then the door clicked shut, and he was gone. Phew! That was my job done for another day. And even though he was late, I'd always catch him stopping outside to admire his reflection and fix his hair in the reflection of our neighbour's car window. It never failed to make me smile. Nothing was more important to him than image, just like most kids his age. He'd fret endlessly about his glasses:

"Do you think I look too geeky? And what about my ears, do I need to flatten them in a little?"

"You're beautiful," I told him. "Geeky and beautiful!"

After school, he'd flop back into bed, exhausted, as though he'd just come back from a mountain expedition. Sometimes, he'd text me or Mum, from his bedroom, to ask for a cold Vimto or a snack.

"This is not a café!" I yelled up the stairs. "There is no waitress service!"

But of course he had a willing little assistant in Raafat, who was nine years old by now, and thought it was a real treat to run up the stairs with a drink or a bag of crisps for his uncle. I'd hear the two of them giggling together upstairs, and it always warmed my heart. It was funny, too, how history seemed to be repeating itself; Yousef adored Mazen and looked up to him; and now Raafat had Yousef on a pedestal too. He had a special bond with Yousef and hung onto his every word. We were more than fortunate, I realised, to have this large and loving family; it was like having a protective buffet between us and the rest of the world. At parents' evening, we were told Raafat was showing exceptional academic ability and we were asked to consider sending him to grammar school, following in Yousef's footsteps. Like Mum, I had many misgivings. But like her, I gave in, and I agreed to let him sit the exam.

"I'll tutor him!" Yousef offered him immediately. "I want to help!"

It was heart-warming, watching them both sitting side by side at the dining table, huddled together over books or an iPad. Yousef was a passionate and innovative teacher, and he kept the lessons light and full of fun. I worried that Yousef was spending too much time with Raafat and not enough on his own studies, but he waved my worries away with his customary confidence.

"I'll be fine," he insisted. "You know me."

It wasn't until around ten days before the start of the GCSE exams that he finally clicked into panic mode.

"I need you to test me," he announced, thrusting a book on Chinese grammar into my hand. Of course I hadn't a clue what he was saying but I nodded along, pretending to be impressed. In that last week before the exams we covered the house with post-it notes, filled with Shakespeare quotes or Physics equations. At each mealtime, Yousef would run through the key features of a motte-and-bailey castle, or the structure of a leaf.

"There's so much to learn," he said in concern. "I'm beginning to wish I'd made more effort."

One night, Yousef took a jar of coffee out of the cupboard and produced some chewing gum.

"I'm going to have to pull an all-nighter," he said dramatically, his face deadly serious, as he dumped his books onto the kitchen table. "This is an emergency."

I chuckled to myself all the way home. Just now, when he thought he was growing up, he was still such a little boy at heart. His idea of extreme behaviour was a night of instant coffee and revision. When I arrived back the next morning to wake him for school, he was still fast asleep with his head on the dining room table.

"Yousef!" I yelled. "You have an exam today!"

He jumped up, disorientated, and then dashed out of the house, nerves jangling from too much caffeine and too little sleep. I peered out of the living room window and caught him briefly checking his hair in the neighbour's car window, as usual.

"Even on exam day, Yousef." I said to myself. "You are nothing if not predictable."

But by now, I had very few concerns about his unorthodox approach. I was expecting great things from him. Given his past successes, I had no doubt at all that he would do well. After each exam, he came home and collapsed into bed, and we had to entice him out and remind him that there were more subjects left to revise.

"More coffee," he said resignedly. "More chewing gum."

By the end of June the exams were over, and he was invited to the leavers' prom, along with all of his friends. Mum took him into Manchester to buy him a suit and that evening, we insisted he tried it on for us. He gave a mini fashion show in the hallway, and we all cheered and wolf whistled as he strutted to the front door and back.

"Are you taking a young lady to the prom?" Mazen asked him.

"I'm taking three!" Yousef winked.

On the night of the prom itself, he emerged from the bathroom, reeking of aftershave, with his hair neatly gelled, his eyes shining with anticipation.

"Is there a Lynx tap in that bathroom?" I spluttered as he came into the living room. "I can smell it halfway down the street."

"I can smell my Armani aftershave too," said Mazen, waggling a jokey finger at him. "Have you been stealing my stuff?"

Yousef nodded and laughed. He hadn't a care in the world.

"Smells better on me anyway," he quipped.

He looked so handsome, so grown-up, that I felt suddenly emotional. Where had my little Yo-Yo gone? The prom night was a brilliant success, and in the days afterwards, with no pressure of exam timetables, he sank back into being a regular teenager; lying in bed late every day, hoovering up the contents of the entire fridge in one sitting, seeing his friends in the evenings. Results day came and Yousef met with his classmates to collect his grades in person, at school. Mum and I waited on tenterhooks at home. When he didn't call or text, we both felt a flicker of unease.

"What if he's failed the lot?" I said, doubts creeping in. "He didn't revise nearly as much as he should have."

But in the next moment, he burst into the house, whooping and screaming with delight.

"I thought I'd leave you in suspense, keep you guessing!" he grinned. "I passed the lot! Grade A in Advanced Maths!"

He had smashed an amazing 11 GCSEs, with Maths, Advanced Maths, English Literature, English Language, Biology, Chemistry, Physics, History and RE at grade A and A-star, a B in Chinese and a C in French.

"Gosh, only a B and a C in languages," I joked. "Yousef, how embarrassing for you!"

We celebrated that night by going to an all-you-can-eat buffet in Manchester – Yousef and Maz's favourite treat. And then we all clubbed together to get him a ticket for Leeds festival too. He went along with his friends and had a wonderful weekend. All through that summer, Yousef played lots of sport and saw his old friends from primary school, as well as his more recent friends from MGS. He took up boxing, joining a boxing gym nearby, really throwing himself into it. According to his coach, who often kindly drove him home after training, he was a promising boxer.

"My coach says he'll enter me for my first fight if I keep on improving," Yousef said excitedly. "I can't wait."

Not for the first time, I was struck by the contrasts in Yousef's life. Every day at school, he rubbed shoulders with the children of millionaire businessmen, whilst at home Mum got by on benefits and a part-time wage. I'd often looked at his long fingers and slim hands and thought how suited he would be to work as a surgeon. Yet now, he was using those same elegant hands to box. He was proud to be English, yet he was appreciative of his Lebanese roots. He was equally at home with the Catholic and Muslim faiths. He was a boy of contradictions and contrasts, of acceptance and peace, but essentially, he was a boy who was open to all possibility; bursting with potential, brimming with aspirations, hungry for new experiences.

He lost almost 20kgs thanks to his new fitness routine and he looked fitter and healthier than ever before. I knew he sneaked the odd cigarette out of his bedroom window, which, he promised me, was his only vice.

"I'm going to give up, now that I'm getting into boxing," he said.

And as he focussed more on sport, he smoked less and socialised less too. He loved shadow boxing his way around the house, trying out his new moves and driving us all crazy. It was a juggling act, trying to pass him on the stairs whilst he boxed imaginary opponents on every step. One time, he completely misjudged his cross and punched a hole in the living room door! Yousef's face fell when he saw how easily the door had cracked.

"Who's going to fix that?" Mum asked, trying to keep her face straight.

"Me!" Yousef promised. "Honestly, I will. I'll get a job and I'll pay to get it fixed."

Both Mum and I knew that was very unlikely to happen. He had £10 per week spending money, which he saved carefully, week by week, to buy the next designer T-shirt or the next must-have pair of joggers. There was no way he'd be spending his money on a new door. And though he kept reassuring us he was looking for a part-time job, it was, as with most teenagers, a suspiciously slow process.

"I'll fix the hole," Mazen volunteered. "Don't worry about it."

He and Yousef exchanged a wink and I had the feeling we'd be keeping the hole for some time to come.

13

During those summer days, Yousef was out all the time, boxing, cycling, or playing football in the park. Sometimes, he'd look after Raafat for me; giving him boxing tutorials in the back garden or teaching him how to cross a football. He was so good with younger children. If the weather was good, he'd take Raafat and the little ones to feed the ducks in the local park, and then for sweets on the way home. He even booked himself and Raafat onto an animation course which was being held at Ladybarn Primary.

"I loved it just as much as Raf did," Yousef told me. "He's such a bright kid Jade, honestly. I can't wait for him to come to MGS. He'll be like my little mini-me."

For sixth form, Yousef was anxious to be allowed to continue his studies at MGS, but he knew that progression wasn't automatic. He had to have an interview and prove himself academically before he could be considered for a place. He seemed more nervous about securing his place at sixth form than he was about his GCSE exams.

"A lot of the regular kids don't get a place," he told me. "I really hope they pick me."

It was an anxious wait. Soon after, a letter came through the post, formally accepting him into the sixth form. He was absolutely elated.

"Yes!" he shouted, punching the air.

He had to wear a suit every day for sixth form which was more expense for Mum, but again, she juggled her finances and somehow found the money. He needed a new tie as well, yellow and red, to mark him out from the younger ones. There was more celebration when his pals, Adam and Yas, were accepted at the MGS sixth form too.

"It couldn't have worked out any better," Yousef said. "Studying A-levels at MGS is my best chance of getting into medical school."

That September, Yousef began studying A-levels in Chemistry, Biology, Maths and Economics. He was in the same classes as Adam and so the two boys were spending more time together. Adam was often round at our house, and Mum commented more than once on his lovely manners.

"Adam loves my cooking," she told me. "He always says please and thank you. He's such a nice boy. Such a good influence."

Yousef celebrated his 17th birthday on September 28, 2018. For months, he had been pleading with Mum to buy him a pair of white Nike trainers, at a cost of around £200. Many of his friends had the same pair, in black.

"I really want them," he wheedled. "I *need* them."

"You'll have to wait until your birthday," Mum told him. "You know the rules."

"All my friends have them," he persisted. "They just went out and bought them with their weekly spends. They don't have to wait for a birthday, like I do."

But Mum stood firm. His big day finally came around, and Ghaleb had bought the trainers and sent them for him. Yousef unwrapped the box and let out a squeal of delight.

"Look!" he beamed, his whole face glowing with pleasure. "Aren't they the coolest pair of trainers you've ever seen?"

To me, they looked like a normal pair of white trainers, but I nodded along; his enthusiasm was catching. We had a party at home for him too; cakes and coke cans and paper plates all over the kitchen. Mum and I surveyed the debris whilst Yousef and his pals played footie in the garden. It was a flashback to his party at the end of primary school.

"The years roll on by and actually, he hasn't changed a bit," Mum smiled. "He's still my little Yo-Yo."

Yousef's first term of sixth form went well. But after his exams, he came home with a long face and flung himself melodramatically onto the sofa.

"Failed them all," he said despairingly. "Every single exam."

Mum and I stared at him, horrified.

"What?" I gulped.

Yousef shrugged sadly.

"Nothing I can do about it now," he said. "I'll have to leave MGS. They're throwing me out."

I gawped at him, torn between astonishment and sympathy that he'd wasted his chances. But then, his cheek twitched a little. And I saw the muscles in his face working up and down. His mouth turned upwards, ever so slightly, with the makings of a smile, and I yelled and threw a cushion at him.

"Yousef, that was so mean of you!" I shouted, as he burst into peals of laughter. "We really believed you! I was almost in tears!"

"Sorry," he laughed. "You two are just so easy to wind up. You're irresistible. I got straight A's, so you can stop panicking."

He had done so well, in fact, that his teachers had recommended him to apply for Oxbridge. He was becoming more focussed too about applying to medical school.

"I'd like to be a surgeon," he told us. "Either a heart surgeon, or a brain surgeon. I want to save lives. I want to find a cure for arthritis. One day, I'll be famous and in all the newspapers."

"I would love that," Mum said.

"And when I get my wages," he said, with a twinkle in his eye. "I'll buy you your very own house, and you can have a chauffeur-driven limousine to Aldi each week."

I laughed and threw my arms around him.

"You've got a heart of gold, Yousef, you know that?" I said.

Christmas Day 2018 dawned, and we all ate a big Christmas lunch together, at Mum's house. Yousef and Maz were kept busy all day slotting batteries into toys and putting Lego figures together. Like most teenage boys, they got lots of chocolate, deodorant, and novelty socks, but the little boy who still shone bright in each of them was far more interested in the Lego and the remote-control fire-engines, than the grown-up gifts. The house was chaotic; noisy, messy and far too warm. But as I looked around my family; Mum, Yousef, Maz, Mazen, Raafat, Zack, and Daniel, I felt a surge of contentment. It was a typical Christmas, but at once a perfect Christmas too. We didn't have much and yet we had absolutely everything. We scrimped for every penny, but we were rich beyond our wildest dreams.

If I had known these were to be our last moments of Christmas happiness, could I have grasped them any tighter?

On New Year's Eve, Yousef went out with his pals from MGS, along with another boy, Joshua Molnar, who I understood was from a different school. On New Year's Day, Yousef slept in late, and my boys eventually lost patience with him and burst into his room, bouncing on his bed to wake him up.

"Uncle Yo-Yo! Get up! It's 2019!" they yelled.

"You're becoming a party animal," I joked. "Your boxing coach would have something to say about this."

As January 2019 rolled around, Mum's health improved a little, and she began volunteering at a local charity shop, helping out a couple of times each week. It was a rewarding job, and she liked the social side of it too. Yousef was really enjoying his A-level studies and Maz was making excellent progress with his GCSE work at school. Sometimes, Mum and I had worried about Maz feeling eclipsed by his brother's shadow, especially since Yousef cast such a bright light. As the older son, Yousef naturally spoke up first, took the responsibility, made the decisions. If Mum needed bread from the shop, she sent Yousef. If someone had to stay home for a parcel, she chose Yousef. Sometimes, Yousef would grumble and try to shirk the task but mostly he relished the trust she placed in him. Yousef was only chosen because he was the older child, as in most families, but we realised that Maz perhaps was a little in his shade. But now with them both at different schools, they seemed to form their own friendships and their own identities and Maz was maturing into a lovely young man in his own right. Separating them both, in education, had been the best thing to do. Mazen and I, meanwhile, had our hands full with our three boys, Raafat, now nine, Zack, nineteen months and baby Daniel, eight months. Life was going well for us all. Sometimes, I felt really lucky; I felt *too* lucky. I had three beautiful children, a wonderful husband, a loving mum and brothers. As a natural worrier, I would sometimes fret that perhaps there was trouble lurking, just around the corner.

"Jade, you have no need to torment yourself," Mazen reassured me. "We're just a normal family, getting on with life. Nothing will go wrong."

Mid-way through February 2019, Yousef went to a Fredo gig in Manchester, with his pal, Adam. Afterwards, they both slept in the living room, with the sofa cushions arranged into makeshift beds on the carpet.

"When I came downstairs during the night, they were both fast asleep," Mum told me later. "Adam had kicked his duvet off, so I tucked him in. They looked so sweet. Still just like little boys, really."

The day after the sleep-over, Adam's mum sent flowers to Mum, probably as a thank you for the way we'd welcomed him into our family. I saw Adam's mum on the pavement, outside the house, as I was on my way to collect Raafat from school.

The following week was February half-term and Mazen and I had saved up to take the children to Lebanon, to visit his family. When we got back, I went straight to Mum's, and Yousef came running into the living room, shouting:

"Where's my lovely sister and my lovely nephews?"

He hugged us all in turn and I laughed.

"What's brought this on?" I asked suspiciously.

"Nothing," he said innocently. "But have you got a spare £2 for boxing please?"

That night, after he had trained at the gym, he waited for Mazen to come home from work, so that they could eat together as usual. And at the dining table, the conversation turned to Yousef's future.

"I'd like to try for Oxbridge, of course I would, but I'm worried about the costs," he told Mazen. "The teachers at MGS have been very helpful, they say there's a lot of support available. They think I might qualify for grants and bursaries. But I'm still not convinced. If it's too expensive, I won't apply, because I don't want Mum to be landed with the costs. She's done enough."

"But think of the benefits of doing medicine at Oxford or Cambridge," Mazen urged him. "You could borrow the money you need in a student loan, and you'd soon earn enough to pay back all the debt."

Yousef nodded thoughtfully.

In the next minute, he was Googling doctors' salaries on his phone.

"Wow, that's more than I thought," he whistled. "I could pay back my loans, and I could get Mum a new house too. Maybe even a little car!"

"I don't even drive anymore!" she reminded him.

"Well, I'll buy you a special mobility car for your arthritis!" he insisted. "Maybe I'll even get you a chauffeur!"

Mum laughed. I was pleased he was thinking of other people, he was becoming a kind and generous young man. But I still worried a little that he was so easily swayed by money, as though it would solve every problem he had.

"He'll grow out of that," Mazen assured me. "All teenage boys are materialistic. It's perfectly natural, especially when he has such wealthy friends. He's going in the right direction, Jade. Don't worry."

But that was my problem. I worried.

14

On the morning of Friday, March 1, 2019, I dropped Raafat at school, and went round to Mum's, as usual, with Zack and Daniel in the double buggy. When I arrived, Maz was busily getting ready for school, but Yousef was still in bed.

"What's wrong with him, is he ill?" I asked.

Mum shook her head and sighed.

"No, I don't think so," she said. "He's just tired. He was boxing down at the gym until late last night, his coach dropped him home about 11pm, and now he just won't get up."

This was typical of Yousef; he loved his boxing so much that he'd train too hard, and then he wanted to sleep for a week afterwards.

"He should go to school," I said firmly.

I went upstairs to remonstrate with him, but he was absolutely zonked, underneath his Manchester United duvet cover.

"He's swinging the lead," I said. "Nothing wrong with him. Chronically lazy. That's my diagnosis."

At around lunchtime, we heard stirrings upstairs and Yousef's face appeared in the kitchen doorway a few moments later.

"Morning!" he said cheerfully, even though it was already afternoon. "Anyone fancy a trip to the shop for a lolly?"

I wanted to be strict with him, but it was impossible. Daniel was having a nap, but Zack's eyes lit up.

"Me!" he shouted. "Me please, Uncle Yo-Yo!"

"Come on Zu-Zu," Yousef grinned, scooping him up in his arms.

Off they went to the corner shop, giggling like two co-conspirators, in search of a 10p lollipop. When they got back, Yousef sat Zack on his knee, and said to me: "You are so lucky to have these children, Jade. So lucky."

I smiled, but it struck me as an odd thing to say. Yousef wasn't an emotional sort of boy, and this was uncharacteristically serious. Despite the sentiment, I was a little unsettled.

"Isn't he cute?" Mum cooed, pinching Yousef's cheek. "To think Jade, we used to change his nappies, not that long ago, and look at the size of him now. He's changing Daniel's nappies instead."

"Stop it, that's too much now," Yousef blushed.

Just then his phone rang, and he took a call from one of his friends. From what I could gather, someone they knew had been in trouble by the Subway shop in Hale Barns, Cheshire, where a lot of his schoolmates lived.

"Don't you get involved, whatever it is," Mum warned him when the call finished.

"I won't, I promise," Yousef replied. "But I'm feeling so much better now. Can I go to Adam's? We're meeting up with some mates and going for a bike ride."

By this time, school had finished, and his friends were obviously making plans for the evening and the weekend.

"I don't think you should go out," I said to him sternly. "You've been off school. If you're not well enough for school, you're not well enough for a bike ride. You should have an early night."

But somehow, Yousef managed to talk Mum round, into letting him go out. Moments later, he dashed past me in the hallway, with his coat on. He was trying to fix his hair with his fingers as he went along.

"How did you wangle that?" I asked.

"It's my natural charm," he replied, as though it should have been obvious.

Normally, Yousef would kiss everyone goodbye, but he was in a rush to catch the tram, so he just shouted: "Goodbye," and then he was gone. The house was suddenly quieter, sadder somehow, and it felt as though the energy and the fun had been sucked out of the room.

"I want Uncle Yo-Yo," Zack shouted.

"He'll be back soon," I promised.

But at 7pm, Yousef texted to ask if he could stay over at Adam's house in Cheshire. That wasn't unusual; he spent a lot of time there.

'That's fine,' Mum texted him back. 'Love you.'

We went home and the next morning, a Saturday, I called Mum, as usual.

"Yousef isn't home yet but I'm expecting him back this evening. It's just me and Maz here today," she said.

That afternoon, I popped round to help out with some housework and we had something to eat with Mum. Then, Mazen and I took the boys home, to get them ready for bed, leaving Mum and Maz at the house. Yousef still wasn't home.

"Yousef just texted, asking me what I'm cooking for dinner," Mum laughed as I was putting the boys' coats on, ready to leave. "Always thinking of his stomach, that boy."

By 8pm, I was lying in bed, next to Zack, trying to settle him to sleep whilst he wriggled and fidgeted and whispered in my ear.

"Sleep time," I murmured. "Close your eyes."

I could see my phone on the bedside table, flashing with a call from Mum, but I ignored it. Zack would never sleep if he knew she was calling; he'd insist on talking to her. But then, I heard her calling Mazen instead. I caught snippets of the conversation, through the bedroom door:

"What is it...have you fallen?...yes I can get there, no problem...which hospital?"

I sprang up in bed, suddenly worried and alert.

"What's going on?" I asked Mazen.

He shook his head, but he seemed worried.

"I don't really know," he said. "Your mum has asked me to meet her at the hospital. I thought maybe she'd had an accident, a fall with her arthritis, but she says not. She says she's fine, and Maz is with her, so I think Yousef might have had an accident."

"What?" I gulped.

"I don't know, Jade," he said again. "I'll get straight there and call you as soon as I have any news."

I felt sick inside. I wanted desperately to go with him, but I couldn't leave the three boys on their own. Mazen drove, and I didn't, so it made sense for him to go alone. After the children were settled, I paced the flat, up and down the living room, staring at my phone and willing Mazen or Mum to call me. The minutes dragged so slowly, and I grew more and more anxious. Why the delay? Then, in the silence, my phone bleeped, and I snatched it up with a jolt. But it was just my friend, Paula.

"How's the diet going?' she texted.

She and I had both joined a slimming club, and I was trying to lose some of my baby weight. We'd send each other little messages of support, especially on a Saturday night when we might be tempted to indulge and have a bag of Maltesers in front of the telly.

'I'm in a bit of a state,' I replied. 'I think Yousef might have been in an accident. Just waiting for Mazen to call from the hospital with more news.'

'I'm coming round,' Paula replied.

She lived on the same street, and moments later, she was knocking on my door. I fell gratefully into her arms for a hug.

"I don't know what's going on," I fretted. "I keep calling Mazen, but his phone is switched off. Mum's too."

The minutes dragged unbearably. The wait was purgatorial, and though Paula did her best to keep my spirits up, all I could think of was Yousef. If it was just a minor accident, a broken arm or a sprained ankle, why had nobody let me know? It was around 10pm when my phone finally rang. I knew, from Mazen's quick, panicked breathing, that this was something more than a fracture, that this was something far more serious.

"Yousef has been stabbed," he said. "We don't know any details. I'm at the hospital with your mum and Maz."

My heart lurched.

"Stabbed? What, do you mean on purpose? Has he been mugged?" I stuttered.

"I don't know, we don't know anything," Mazen replied. "I'm sorry. Look, just try to rest and I will be home as soon as I can."

He sounded as though he was fighting back tears as he hung up and I had a horrible, sloshing feeling in the bottom of my stomach. Every pore in my body tingled as the anxiety shrink-wrapped around me. I could smell the fear, I could taste it. I could feel its fingers stroking my face. I tried hard to breathe slowly and deeply but I felt so much worse now than before Mazen had called.

"Yousef has been stabbed," I repeated to myself. "We don't know any details. How can someone be stabbed, out of nowhere, and for no reason?"

Eventually, I persuaded Paula to go home. She had her own family to think of.

"It's late," I said. "I'll be fine, really, Mazen will be in touch soon."

But my mind was whirring with alarm. What did he mean, *stabbed?* And was it serious? It certainly sounded it. I thought about calling the hospital myself, but something held me back. For whatever reason, Mazen wanted me to wait for his call. I had to trust in him.

"Come on Mazen," I fretted. "Call me, please."

At just after midnight, my phone rang for a second time.

"Jade, I'm so sorry," Mazen began. "I don't know how to say this…I'm so sorry."

All of a sudden, I heard a loud whoosh in my ears, and a screaming sound inside my head, drowning out my husband's voice. I knew what was coming. I didn't want to hear it. I couldn't listen to it. I wanted to clap my hands around my ears and smash my phone against the wall.

"He's dead," Mazen sobbed. "Yousef is gone."

My knees buckled and I sank down onto the carpet. It seemed as though all my bones had turned to liquid. I felt my chest go tight as I snatched at each breath; it was like all the oxygen had been sucked out of the room. I was giddy with the shock. I wanted to ask Mazen if there might be some mistake, if he was absolutely sure, but the words all dried and shrivelled in my mouth and there was no sound, save for Mazen quietly sobbing.

"I'll be home as soon as I can," he whispered eventually. He ended the call, but it barely registered with me.

My vision went blurry and jagged as tortuous images of Yousef swam across my eye-line; 17-year-old Yousef dashing out of the house just hours earlier: *It's my natural charm!'* Yousef at 16 teaching Raafat how to box in the back garden: *'Jab, cross, hook!'* Yousef, aged 11, sitting on the stage on his first day at MGS, with his whole, brilliant life stretched out ahead of him like a glittering red carpet: *'I'm going to love it here!'*

I could not believe that I would never see those beautiful brown eyes again.

For hours I lay slumped on the floor, stock-still, ossifying, and frozen in a stupor. There were no tears, I could not allow myself to cry, because that would be accepting that he was dead. At 4am, I heard the familiar click of Mazen's key in the front door, but though I was desperate to see him, I was also desperate not to see him. I couldn't bear to hear him say it out loud.

"I'm so sorry," he whispered, and he took me in his arms.

"No," I said defiantly, angrily almost. I wanted to push him away, send him back outside and make him come in with a different outcome, a different opening gambit.

"No," I hissed, through gritted teeth. "There must be some mistake."

I was relying on Mazen, pinning all my hopes on him, that there might have been some administrative error, some misunderstanding, and that it was another family, not ours, who had lost a boy. In that moment, I wished our tragedy on someone else. My love and affection for Yousef had made me selfish and heartless. It was the cruellest paradox.

"It must be someone else," I repeated desperately, clutching at each word as though through a thick fog. "It's not Yousef."

But Mazen shook his head. Through his sobs, he told me that he had seen Yousef in the morgue with his own eyes, and that yes, he was gone and there was no doubt and no mistake. My beloved brother was dead.

"I wasn't allowed to touch his body, but I was able to wipe his face clean and fix his hair, just the way he likes it," Mazen stuttered, his voice no more than a whisper.

He pulled a small scrap of cloth from his pocket, which was crumpled and blood-stained.

"I made him look smart and handsome," he said, straightening the cloth out, carefully, reverently. "And peaceful too."

I clung to that crumb of comfort; that image of Mazen gently cleaning Yousef's cheeks and gelling back his hair. It was as though, by attending to his personal grooming, which had been so important to him, we could somehow keep him alive. By gelling his hair, we could maybe wake him up.

"What happened?" I asked. "Who killed him? And why? Why would anyone want to hurt Yousef?"

I had a million questions swarming around my head, but Mazen couldn't answer any of them.

"I knew that Yousef was dead, that first time I called you," he confessed. "He was dead before he even arrived at the hospital. But I just couldn't bring myself to tell you. When it came to it, I couldn't break your heart. I'm so sorry, Jade."

Outside of my own cloud of grief, I could see that Mazen was completely overwhelmed too. He'd had to call Ghaleb, and all of our relatives in Lebanon, to break the news of Yousef's death. He was making calls to Mum's family members, all around Manchester. He was standing strong, for my sake and for Mum, but he was crumpling and breaking inside, just as I was.

He continued: "All I know is that Yousef had suffered a single stab wound to the heart. He died either at the scene or on the way to hospital."

Each word sliced through me; a wound through my own heart.

"The police have opened a murder investigation, but they can't tell us anything really at this stage," he said. "He must have been mugged and attacked by a stranger. Did he have any money with him or anything which might single him out to be attacked?"

I tried to think back to the Friday evening. Yousef had left the house in such a rush, but I remembered he had been wearing his prized white trainers, his Zara bubble coat and some ordinary joggers, no big names, no fancy labels.

"I can't imagine that anyone would mug him for his trainers," I said. "All the kids have them. They're just Nike trainers."

Mazen nodded in agreement.

Yousef had a silver signet ring. But again, it was only cheap; it was just something he liked, it had no great value. Certainly it was not a reason to mug or stab him. The most valuable thing he had was probably his iPhone. I wondered whether he'd been attacked for that, but again, all the kids had those phones.

"Where did it happen? Was it in a particularly rough part of the city centre?" I asked.

Mazen shook his head.

"The paramedics found him on a street in Hale Barns," he said. "One of the wealthiest streets in the whole of the North-West."

I stared at him, unable to process this new minor shock, on top of the avalanche of trauma and pain. I was buried under it all.

"Hale Barns! How could he have been stabbed in a place like that?" Mazen shrugged helplessly. We were both feeling our way in the dark. Both out of our depth.

"So he must have been with Adam then," I reasoned, trying to focus on a train of thought. "Adam lives in Hale Barns. He will know what happened. We should call him. He'll be able to tell us what went wrong."

In that instant, I whispered a silent prayer that Adam was with Yousef, in his final moments; that he looked upon the face of someone he held dear as he snatched at his final seconds on this earth. I had a sudden grotesque image of Yousef flailing; clinging desperately to the last lingering breaths of life and I retched and dashed to the bathroom. Yousef was young and strong and indestructible. How could he now have died on a strange street, in mysterious circumstances?

"We need to call Adam," I repeated.

"Yes," Mazen agreed. "But first, let's go to your mum and Maz. They need us the most."

15

At 6am, we woke the children and got them dressed, going through a familiar routine which by now felt alien and woefully unsuitable. Inside my head, the news screamed relentlessly on a loop: 'Yousef is dead! Yousef is dead!'

"Come on," I said gently, herding the children into the bathroom to brush their teeth. "Time for a new day."

There would be no new day for Yousef. He would never clean his teeth again, never sleep through his alarm, never run for the school bus. Never. I felt dizzy and unglued, as though parts of me were chipping away and floating off. I knew I would never get them back.

"Why?" I pleaded. "Why?"

But there was nobody to ask and nobody to reply.

I spooned Weetabix into Zack's baby-bird mouth, and watched his eyes light up with glee as he managed to grab a handful and rub it into his hair. And yet in my mind, all I could see was a picture of Yousef stabbed and dying, gargling and choking on his own blood. The two scenes, juxtaposed, were completely absurd and incongruous. I was persuaded, again, to think that there might be some mistake, that maybe Mazen had visited the wrong body. But then, through the jumble of my thoughts, I heard him in the next room, softly breaking news of the tragedy to Raafat.

"Uncle Yousef can't be with us any longer," he said. "I'm so sorry. You won't see him again, but you can still talk to him in your heart."

Raafat covered his little face and the tears flowed. At nine years old, he understood little of the magnitude of the tragedy, and certainly not the permanence of it. I knew that in time, the agony would hurt him all the more.

"How will we live without him?" he wept. "Everyone loves Uncle Yo-Yo."

I cradled him in my arms, and we cried together.

"Uncle Yo-Yo is in a good place now," I told him. "You have to remember that he loved you, and Zack, and Daniel, very much."

We arrived at Mum's at just after 7am. The front door was ajar, and she was in her usual armchair, yet this morning, she didn't seem to fill it in quite the same way. She looked smaller and somehow out of shape, as though grief had physically changed and diminished her, leaving her a mere shell of her usual lively self.

"Mum," I said weakly. "Mum."

I just couldn't find the right words. I went to hug her, gently, but she did not respond or soften in the way she usually would. Holding her in my arms, I felt she might crack; physically and emotionally, that we might all disintegrate under the impossible weight of our suffering. There is no greater loss, no sharper or more destructive pain, than for a mother to lose a child. It is something, from the moment we give birth, that we all fear and dread. And now that it had happened to my own mother, I knew that a part of her was irredeemably and irreversibly lost. Yet not lost. For Yousef had been taken from us. He had been stolen. He had left the house fit, healthy and glowing with life. Now, he was lying on a cold slab with a hole torn through his heart.

Before 9am, two police liaison officers, Kath and Caroline, arrived at Mum's. They repeated what we already knew; that Yousef had been stabbed to death on a leafy street in Cheshire, near to where many of his friends lived, at around 6.30pm the previous evening. They had no more details.

"Yousef's death is already being discussed online," they warned. "We've had requests from the press for a photo of Yousef to use alongside the reports into his death. What do you think?"

Mum and I stared blankly. We didn't know what we thought. We couldn't process anything beyond the fact that Yousef was not here at home as he should be. We'd never had dealings with the press or the police in our entire lives.

"Look, the press will get hold of a photo from somewhere," said Kath. "Especially for a boy of Yousef's age, it is so easy to find a photo on social media. We want this to be your choice and under your control. If you supply the picture, it gives you some input."

I thought, in that moment, of the lovely photo we had of Yousef in his prom suit. He had looked so handsome, so full of promise and passion for the future. His future. He had been stressed out, as usual, over his glasses: *Do I look too geeky?'* and his ears: *'Does one ear stick out more than the other?'* And we had all said: *'Yousef, you look a million dollars!'* and he had beamed and basked in the certainty of our love.

I gave Kath the prom photo and a silly and desperate part of me expected her to smile and comment on what a fine young man he was. I didn't want this to be his death photo. Kath emailed the picture to the various media outlets and within an hour, Yousef's name and picture was flashing up on news feeds from all around the UK. I could hear his voice, in the background, in the kitchen maybe, telling us:

'I'm going to be famous, I'll be in all the newspapers!'

And there was his devoted primary school teacher too, who had promised us that Yousef's work on rockets would stay on the classroom wall, long after he'd left, because he believed he was going to be celebrated and famous in some way. But not in this way. This was not what he had in mind. I thought of his teacher, and of all his teachers, his friends, his boxing coaches, his football team, all enjoying Sunday morning coffee and scrolling lazily through the news feeds before seeing the shocking story of Yousef's death online. Even then, outside of my own mourning, I could appreciate that Yousef's passing would have deep and wounding ramifications right across the city. He was our boy, but he was loved by so many.

'17-year-old boy stabbed to death!'

'Named by police as Yousef Ghaleb Makki.'

'Two other boys, both also aged 17, remain in police custody on suspicion of his murder.'

It seemed so inappropriate, so intrusive, seeing Yousef's smile staring back at me from a long list of websites. He hadn't even been dead for 24 hours yet. And it also felt as though Yousef didn't matter; his life, his death, laid bare in the media for all to see; errors, spelling mistakes, sweeping assumptions. In life, he had been the boy with the most dazzling future ahead of him. In death, I felt he was afforded no dignity or respect. It broke my heart all over again.

"Who are the two 17-year-olds in custody?" I asked the liaison officers.

But they couldn't tell me. It didn't occur to me for a single minute that, at 17, the same age as Yousef, they might be known to him. They might be his peers. Less still, his friends. I thought the age factor was purely coincidence.

Mid-morning, the doorbell started to ring, with concerned neighbours, friends, and relatives, all arriving with flowers and cards and messages of sympathy. As I went to answer the door, I tripped over Yousef's school bag and shoes in the hallway, and instinctively, I scooped them up, to put them away. But away where? The realisation smacked me full in the face that Yousef would never carry this bag again. He would never wear these shoes. He wouldn't finish his homework, sit his exams, become a brain surgeon. He wouldn't admire his hair in the mornings. He wouldn't leave crisp packets under the bed. Mum caught sight of me holding the bag and called:

"Put those back in the hallway please, they belong to Yousef."

There was a hysteria to her voice, a lack of control, which made me stack them neatly at the side of the hallway without challenge. And perhaps if we kept his bag here, he'd come back for it? Was Mum thinking the same as I was? I oscillated violently between believing Yousef was dead to convincing myself that he was on his way home. There was no middle ground and how could there be?

The steady stream of visitors continued, and I traipsed wordlessly back and forth from the living room, standing in the doorway, arms hanging uselessly by my side, like a broken puppet. "Thank you, thank you," I mumbled, but each syllable was like a razor blade through the side of my mouth. It was so painful; just to speak.

Mid-morning, Rachel arrived, having driven over five hours from her home in Devon. Yousef had been killed on her 33rd birthday. "Jade," she wept, and we fell into each other's arms.

Ghaleb travelled too, from his new home in London, and he fainted as he arrived at the door, overcome with shock. Mazen helped him inside and settled him on the sofa, whilst he came round.

"My son, my son," he wailed. "Where is he?" Like me, he was searching for an alternative, a way out, a miracle.

Meanwhile, more well-wishers came and soon the house was strewn with flowers. Amongst all the sympathy bouquets were the flowers from Adam's mother, bought two weeks earlier as a thank you after the boys' night out. They were still quite fresh and unseemly though it was, they had outlived Yousef himself. I stared at them and wondered again why Adam and his family hadn't been in touch. Later we were told that the police had told them not to contact us but at the time, it was hard to understand.

"It doesn't make sense," I said to Rachel. "Adam was practically his best friend, and they were together yesterday. Adam must know something."

Mum was putting on a show, chatting and smiling and welcoming everyone in, as though this was perhaps a birthday or a party of some kind. But behind the mask, I could see that she was perilously close to collapse. She was in complete denial. She hadn't yet allowed herself to admit that Yousef was gone, that her son was dead, and I wondered whether she ever truly would.

"Enough," I said eventually. "We can't cope with any more visitors. I know they mean well, but this isn't the right time."

We didn't answer the door again. People left bouquets on the doorstep, and I hoped they understood that we were at breaking point. But then a crowd of reporters and photographers turned up, knocking on the door, pushing notes through the letterbox. Even when we turned them away, they camped out in the street. Unsteady with shock, Mum made it to the back garden for a cigarette and as she leaned in the doorway, a photographer sneaked down the alleyway, alongside our house, to snatch a photo of her.

"Please!" she shouted. "Leave us alone!"

She was trembling when she came back indoors. Mazen locked the doors and closed the curtains.

"Don't go in the back garden," he warned. "Don't even take the bin out."

It was probably only one unscrupulous photographer, one bad apple in the whole press pack. But he made us feel as though we were under siege, as though we had done something wrong. We shut ourselves in the living room like prisoners, and, whilst the TV blared in an effort to occupy the children, I focussed on trying to find out what had happened to Yousef. Illogically, I felt that if I could find out the sequence of events, I would somehow be able to start reversing the process, and we might be able to get him home. Mum had by now phoned around to try and get some answers from people who knew Yousef. "Can we call Adam's family?" I asked the liaison officers. "He was with Yousef, he's a good friend, he will know the details."

But one of the officers shook her head.

"It's not a good idea to call anyone who is helping with the investigation at this stage," she replied. "We need to let the police do their job."

It didn't make any sense to me, I just couldn't understand why Adam would be involved in the investigation, but I didn't question it. I had so many other thoughts fighting for space in my head. Instead, I looked online, and examined the social media accounts of Yousef's friends, to see if I could find any clues there. Yousef's death was being widely reported and discussed on social media and, whilst it was upsetting, I tried to look past that, for information. To my surprise, there were lots of comments mentioning Adam and also Joshua Molnar; the boy whose name rang a vague bell, but who I didn't know at all. When I asked Mum, her face was blank. She didn't know Joshua Molnar either. But according to Yousef's friends, they had both been with Yousef when he was attacked.

"What's this about?" I asked the police. "Were the boys there?"

But again, they couldn't say. This made it all the more puzzling why neither of them had been in touch with us. If they had information, or details, then surely, they could understand that we needed to hear them?

"Really, we have to let the investigation team do their job," said the liaison officer. "I know it's hard, but you need to wait for them to release the information to you."

I nodded. I didn't mean to be purposely defiant, but I found myself unable to simply sit and wait and fester. The rogue thoughts began again too; 'What if it's a mistake, what if he's not really dead, what if he's unconscious in a different hospital…?'

My mind was the setting for a screaming, raging, confrontation.

"Can we see Yousef?" I asked eventually. "I need to see him. I need to know for myself that he's gone."

But even as the liaison officer was making arrangements for us to visit his body, I kept my eye on the front window, scanning the street, just in case, just in case… I imagined him dashing up the path, stopping briefly but essentially to check his hair in a car window, falling through the front door in a rush with his trademark:

'I'm starving, Mum! What's for dinner?'

But I waited and waited. And my Yousef did not come. I had seen him, just 40 hours earlier, and he had been heartbreakingly, breathtakingly, alive; each blood vessel pumping, each organ at optimum performance. He was so vital. So vibrant. How could all of that life just stop? Where would it all go?

"You can visit your brother this afternoon," the liaison officer announced. "I will come with you."

16

A short time later, Mazen, Rachel and I were driven to a morgue in Oldham, Greater Manchester, where Yousef's body was being kept. My first thought, bizarrely, as we got into the car, was: 'Oldham? He knows nobody in Oldham, he won't like it there.'

It was around a half hour journey, and I hated the thought of him being so far away. I took Zack and Daniel along with me, but Raafat and Maz stayed at home with Mum. Poor Rachel was suffering from shock; she had been on a birthday night out when Mum called her with the news of Yousef's passing. Minutes later, she was in the car, travelling north, with her life in tatters.

"I can't believe it," she said, as we drove through unfamiliar streets into Oldham. "I keep thinking they've got the wrong boy."

"Me too," I whispered.

The morgue, as we walked inside, was eerily silent.

'Well, what did you expect? A party?' whispered Yousef's cheeky voice in my ear and despite everything, I smiled.

He could still cheer me up, even now – especially now. In front of us was a reception desk, which was deserted and in semi-darkness. It was a sinister place, cold, impersonal, and completely without character, and not the sort of place I wanted for Yousef. *'Well what sort of morgue would you want for me? Honestly, sis!'* Ahead of us lay a long corridor with shiny floor tiles and Zack wriggled down from my arms and ran full length down the passageway, yelling in excitement. The noise and enthusiasm were so incongruous with the ghastly quiet of the morgue; it was odd to have so much life inside a house of death. Yet I knew Yousef, more than anyone, would appreciate the sound of Zack's little shoes on the tiles, and his high-pitched voice babbling with unintelligible excitement.

"I'm afraid you can't touch Yousef because of the murder investigation," said Caroline, the liaison officer who had travelled with us. "Only his face."

I braced myself and closed my eyes as we walked into the room where he was lying. But when I opened them again, he just looked as though he was asleep. His hair was gelled neatly, just as Mazen had promised, and his face was clean, with his stubble showing through. He was as gorgeous and well-groomed as ever. It all fed into my fantasy that this wasn't real, and I half expected him to leap up:

'Prank! Got you again, sis!'

Could this be another one of his jokes? Crazy though it sounds, I clawed at that possibility and waited, with my whole life on pause, willing him to jump up, open an eye, and burst into giggles. But the minutes slid by, and nothing happened. He was still. So still. I could hear Zack shouting and grizzling outside with Mazen, and I knew I couldn't stay in here forever. My life had to go on, unlike

Yousef's. When I leaned over, to kiss him goodbye, his cheek was so cold. It sent a shiver right down my spine. I knew I'd never forget how icy cold he felt. Outside, in the reception area, Caroline handed over Yousef's glasses, and the contents of his pockets. There was the silver ring which he always wore and then, quite unbelievably, a single pound coin.

"Yes," she said, seeing my expression.

"He had just one pound coin in his pocket."

I rolled it around in my hand and the metaphor almost brought me to my knees in anguish. I felt like sinking to the floor and pounding the tiles with my fists in sheer fury and disbelief. My brother, who had transcended his humble background to attend an elite school and mix with the sons of millionaires, had been killed with a solitary pound coin in his pocket. It was just a pound, no more, and yet it was so much more. It was at once worthless and priceless; nothing and everything. I vowed to keep it safe forever.

On the journey home, I wondered again why Adam hadn't been in touch. The longer this went on, the more it just didn't make sense. The next day was Monday. We'd stayed with Mum overnight, not that any of us slept at all. In the dark, it was not helpful, I knew, to dwell on Yousef's last moments but I did not choose to. It was thrust upon me, forced upon me, and in the dead of night I screamed silently, as I imagined the drip, drip of the blood from his wound and the gasp, gasp of his final breath. I was desperate for morning to come, so that the children's incessant chatter would fill this horrible and unrelenting silence. By Monday morning, Mum was sinking into an almost catatonic state of shock. The GP had been to see her and had prescribed some medication, sedatives I imagine, but there was no cure for the pain she was in. I thought of Yousef, poring over the blister pack of tablets, quickly googling the name. *'Wow, bad side effects, are you sure you want to take these, Mum? You might feel better after a bottle of water and a walk around the park. That's Dr Yousef giving you good advice right there.'*

I knew, instinctively, that I had to step up now and I had to be strong for Mum. All my life, I'd turned to her to resolve problems, to take control, to be in charge. She was the focal point of our family, and she was our sun; we took our warmth and our energy from her. Now, it was my turn to look after her and keep her warm.

"Mum, try to eat," I coaxed her. "At least have a cup of tea. And a shower, maybe?"

But she just stared, blankly, right through me. She wouldn't move out of her chair. I tried again and again, offering her toast, hot drinks, a snuggly blanket. And I found that by pretending to cope, I actually could cope. Mum needed me. Maz needed me. My three boys needed me. They were a lifeline; a wonderful distraction and a pacifying antidote during those hours after Yousef's death, keeping us busy and forcing us to continue with a day that none of us wanted to face. I still had to cook, change nappies, wash clothes, and read stories.

"Mummy! Come and see my painting!"

"Can we have a bubble bath, Mummy?"

"When are we going to the park?"

And even though my bones felt weary and leaden, and my heart was bruised and swollen, I was eternally grateful that I had a reason to carry on. So thankful too that my precious little chickens were safe. Yousef's death had taught us all that happiness could be stolen away in a nano-second and that grief could slither in and smother and suffocate us all, like a thick, damp fog.

Poor Maz had been mostly in his bedroom since Yousef's death, but that Monday he was tempted out by Raafat and Zack, who wanted to play with him. Again, I gave thanks that the children were keeping him afloat too.

"Take us to the shop for a lolly!" they pleaded and Maz, though he looked disorientated with sheer misery, nodded and forced a smile.

"Let me find my trainers," he mumbled. "I'll take you now."

Whilst the children were running around with Maz, I picked up some of Yousef's schoolbooks from the dining table and took them upstairs to his bedroom. As I peered around the door, I felt my heart splinter and fracture. There was a can of coke, on his desk, half-full no doubt, probably with his breath still on it. Mum had always complained that he wasted drinks around the house. I could hear him now.

'I'll drink it later! Chill out!'

But of course he never did. There was his bed too, with the football duvet, crumpled and unmade.

'I'm too old for this duvet, and the curtains! My mates will laugh at me! I am not a baby! I'm 17!!!'

I could almost taste the thick miasma of cheap after-shave, sweaty socks, and sneaky cigarettes out of the bedroom window. As I stepped into his room, drawn in by the promise, by the nostalgia, Mum appeared at the bottom of the stairs, where she could see Yousef's doorway.

"Please don't go in his room," she said softly. "I don't want anyone to touch it. I can't bear it."

I wondered if she was hanging on, like me, fooling herself that he might come home. I had seen him in the morgue, ice cold and unmoving, and yet still I clung to that crazy self-preserving notion that he might perhaps come bounding through the door at any moment:

'Sorry! Bus was late and I'm starving! Any chicken wings ready, Mum?'

I even checked in the back garden, just in case he was hiding there. He and Maz had loved playing hide and seek in the garden when they were younger. His basketball hoop hung against the wall, dejected. There was a lonely football poking out from behind a plant. But there was no Yousef.

"Where are you?" I pleaded.

Disconsolate, I stared out at the garden, and had a sudden flashback to one sunny evening over summer 2018. Yousef was out with his pals and had promised to be home by 8pm. Mum, Maz and I were sitting in the garden with the children.

"It's ten past eight," Mum said, checking her watch. "Yousef isn't home. It's not like him."

She gave him another five minutes and then called his phone. No reply. I tried him. No answer. Mum messaged his friends, who assured her he'd left them ages ago, so that he could be home in time. Mum's face blanched.

"What if he's had an accident?" she gasped. "He might have been knocked down. Or abducted even!"

"I don't think so," I said. "Let's stay calm. He'll turn up soon."

But the minutes dragged by and there was no sign of Yousef. We called his phone. We shouted his name around the house and in the street.

"I'm calling the police," Mum said eventually. "It's after 9pm. I think he's been in an accident."

I felt sick inside as Mum dialled 101. But then, from upstairs, we heard Maz shouting and laughing.

"Guess what!" he yelled. "Yousef is here, flat out in bed."

Mum and I stared at each other in astonishment and raced up the stairs; Mum frantically apologising to the police officer on the other end of the phone. Sure enough, there was Yousef, absolutely fast asleep in bed. He had been there the whole time. It was incredible. During our search, I'd had just a cursory look in his room, popped my head around the door. The scrunched-up duvet looked as though there was nobody underneath. I hadn't really expected that he would come home and go upstairs without telling us, so I didn't investigate further.

"Where have you been?" I shrieked, shaking his shoulder. "We've all been worried sick."

Yousef yawned.

"I came home at 8pm, but I was exhausted, so I went straight to bed."

There was a beat of silence and then we all burst out laughing.

"You're safe now," Mum smiled, pulling him in for a hug. "That's all that counts."

He was safe then. But he was not safe now. He would never be safe again.

17

The press camped outside all day, like unwanted stalkers, watching our every move. Mum even asked Rachel, who was a hairdresser, to dye her hair a darker shade of brown, so that she wouldn't be so easy to recognise. That night, again at Mum's house, I hardly slept, drifting in and out of snippets of nightmares so realistic that they left me frozen with terror yet soaked with sweat. In one dream, Yousef came home, his coat zipped up against the cold, a rebellious curl bobbing slightly out of place onto his forehead. But as he staggered in through the door, I realised he was bleeding and bent double in pain.

"I did my best, but I couldn't hang on," he gasped. "Tell the boys I'm sorry."

I reached out to him, both arms outstretched, but he dissolved the second I touched him; he just melted into the background of our cream hallway. Only his white trainers were left behind.

In another dream, the police liaison officers announced that there had been a big mix-up at the morgue and that Yousef wasn't dead after all.

'You can come and collect him,' they told us.

"I knew it!" I told them triumphantly. "I knew it all along!"

We ran around the house in a state of excitement, strapping the children into their car seats and finding everyone's coats and shoes. I dashed into the morgue, where Yousef was being kept, where Zack had raced up and down the corridors, and I was smug with self-congratulation. I had been right all along! But as the door swung open, the room was completely empty. I looked everywhere for him, under tables, in cupboards, down corridors, but he was gone. And when I woke from each terrifying dream, the reality hit me, again and again. There was a tidal wave of teeth-chattering shock each time I regained consciousness. Yousef was gone.

A grey Tuesday morning dawned, and I suggested to Maz and Raafat that it might be a good idea for them to go back to school. The house was weighed down with an oppressive silence and a sadness. It was damaging for the children and I wanted a break for them, however temporary, from the stress.

"Yes," Maz agreed. "I'd like to see my friends."

Raafat felt the same. The schools weren't far away, and we usually walked but I couldn't face seeing and speaking to people, to school mums and to neighbours, although I knew they all meant well. I felt like any small kindness would be enough to break me, and for Mum's sake, and for the children, I couldn't afford to snap. Not now. Instead, Mazen drove them both to school and I turned my attentions to looking after Mum and the little ones. But before lunchtime, I got a call from the teachers at both schools. The boys had to come home; they were inconsolable in class and couldn't continue.

The liaison officers arrived again and this time they had endless questions for us. They wanted to know all about Yousef, from being a baby, right through to his death, and in particular the details of those days before he had died. Mum was in no fit state to answer; she was hardly lucid. She didn't seem to understand what was going on. I did my best to answer everything, but it felt so invasive, as though I was under the spotlight, as though I had done something wrong.

"Can't you tell me what's happening with the investigation?" I pleaded.

But the answer was always the same. I understood that it was important not to prejudice the case. But it was so frustrating too; I felt as though we were being kept in the dark, as though we were under scrutiny in some way. If we, as his closest family, did not qualify for information, then who did? For 17 years, he had been our boy. We had changed his nappies, kissed his grazed knees, cheered his basketball matches. Now, suddenly, when he needed us most, he was no longer considered ours.

"I need to know," I said again. "I have to know who was arrested and why."

Again I turned to social media for information, and I found more comments. This time they were claiming that Joshua Molnar and Adam Chowdhary were the two 17-year-olds arrested in connection with the tragedy.

"I don't believe it," I choked. "How could they be involved? They were his friends."

Adam was one of Yousef's closest friends too. I read and re-read the comments, with my heart thumping. I needed to know and yet at the same time, I didn't want the answers. I was beginning to wonder whether I had been monu-mentally naive; Yousef had been out with his 17-year-old friends. Two 17-year-olds had been arrested following his death. It had not seemed probable, or even possible, to me, that they could be one and the same.

In the end, I texted our liaison officer, who had by now left us for the day.

'Is it true that Joshua and Adam have been arrested?' I asked.

'Yes, it is.'

Three little words pinged right back at me. They scorched through me; a grenade lobbed, with precision, right into the quiet of our living room. I let my phone fall to the floor, and I covered my face with my hands, trying to take in the enormity of what this meant.

It was unthinkable to lose Yousef at the age of 17. Intolerable that he had met a violent death at the hands of a stranger. Monstrous that he had met a violent death allegedly at the hands of a friend.

I thought of Yousef and his wide, trusting eyes and it felt like a clamp on my heart. I knew I had to tell Mum before she heard it from someone else. But the words stuck in my throat as though they might throttle me.

"Mum, the police are questioning his friends," I stuttered. "Joshua and Adam. They're the two 17-year-olds who were arrested on suspicion of murder."

Mum stared right through me for a moment; unseeing, uncomprehending.

"No," she whispered. "Please, no."

I put my arms around her, but she felt unfamiliar and far away, as she had from that first day, when we lost Yousef. Each new horror seemed to chip away at her, and I felt like I was losing her. She was retreating into herself, injured and broken. Her spirit was dying. In those days, I knew, but could not admit, that I had lost my mother as well as my brother.

On March 6, Joshua Molnar appeared before the youth courts in Manchester charged with murdering Yousef, perverting the course of justice and possession of a knife. Adam Chowdhary was charged with perverting the course of justice, possession of a knife, and conspiracy to rob. The charges were as baffling as they were appalling. I didn't understand how the offences of perverting the course of justice or conspiracy to rob applied to Yousef's death at all. Neither boy could be named, by law, in the media, and we read about their brief court appearances online. Yousef was described as 'an *aspiring* heart surgeon' who '*was* a loving and caring son' who '*had* won a scholarship.' It was all in the past. Yousef was in the past. These boys, whatever they faced, still had a future. Yousef did not.

The days afterwards were blurry, each indistinct from the next. The comments and speculation surrounding Yousef's death continued online and led to the police writing to all schools in the area warning pupils to stop discussing the case. I understood it was important not to prejudice the forthcoming trial, but I was also eager for witnesses to come forward and share information that might help. I felt the stern approach from the police might frighten people into staying silent. From the liaison officers, we learned that the murder charge was not clear cut. Joshua Molnar had admitted holding the knife which killed Yousef, but he was apparently claiming self-defence.

"And of course Yousef isn't here to tell us what happened," I said bitterly. "We will never get to hear his account."

The liaison officers came almost every day to Mum's house, asking further questions to build up a picture of Yousef, and I tried to remind myself that they were on our side. But their tone seemed to become more judgemental, at times even accusing. They seemed like double agents; ostensibly offering us support but simultaneously digging for clues.

"Did you ever see Yousef with knives or weapons?"

"Did he drink to excess?"

"No, no, no," I replied. "Nothing like that. He'd have a few drinks with his pals occasionally, I'm sure. He had a secret cigarette out of the bedroom window when Mum was out. But he had never been in any trouble in his life. He was such a good boy."

The police even came to search Yousef's bedroom, which was gut-wrenching for us all, and especially so for Mum. She wanted his room left untouched, unsullied, yet instead it was pulled apart and ransacked as though we had been burgled. It felt worse than a burglary. It was a violation.

"Is this really necessary?" Mazen asked the police, polite but deeply upset. "What exactly are you looking for?"

The officers left empty handed and later, the liaison officers told us that an allegation had been made by one or both of the defendants that Yousef had a knife.

"No!" I gasped immediately. "That's a lie. He's never had a knife. He's a boxer, a sportsman. He has excellent discipline. He wants to be a doctor, a surgeon. He wouldn't carry a knife.

"He's always said to us how he never understood people who carried knives or guns."

The officer nodded.

"Don't worry," she reassured me. "There is no evidence here that Yousef had a knife. Nothing at all. But we had to check. That's our job."

I understood that but it was still unpalatable. The more I found out, the more astounded I became. I was discovering information myself too; both from social media and from lots of Yousef's friends, who visited the house to pay their respects. One told me that a security guard had tried to help Yousef as he lay dying in the road, waiting for an ambulance to arrive. *The Daily Mail* ran the same story too:

'David Beckham's former bodyguard has revealed how he desperately tried to save the life of an A-star private school student stabbed to death on Saturday night.

'Paul Hughes said Yousef Makki, 17, 'looked like a small child' as he lay dying in the street in Hale Barns, Manchester.

'Recalling his frantic attempts to revive the boy, Mr Hughes, who worked with the Beckhams for 12 years, said: 'We laid Yousef on the road, so he was flat and tried to make him as comfortable as possible.

'We put him in the recovery position, tried to do what we could for him, but it wasn't enough. Unfortunately, it was too serious. It must have gone straight through his heart or lungs.'

Mr Hughes went on to say that he had a defibrillator and had tried to give him first aid but there was nothing he could do because the wound to Yousef's chest was so serious.

"I'd like to speak to this man," I said.

His description of Yousef as like 'a small child' had a profoundly sorrowful effect on me. For though he was a big strapping teenager, a boxer, a gifted student, a future surgeon, he was, in essence, still my baby brother. He was still, at 17, just a child. Part of me recoiled at the superficial way in which the media looped in David Beckham, making the story about his celebrity and not about Yousef at all. But a part of me knew also that Yousef would be so thrilled: *'David Beckham's bodyguard tried to save my life! Oh wow!'*

The next day, Mazen and I drove out to Hale, Cheshire, which was around 10 miles away from our home. As we drew nearer to the spot where Yousef had died, I was overawed by the sheer wealth which glared at us from every angle; sweeping driveways leading to multi-million pound mansions, nestling smugly behind the anonymity of electric gates: Keep out! We don't want your sort round here! And behind the gates and high, manicured hedges, were rows and rows of windows; blank, expressionless, and giving nothing away. Further back, I caught glimpses of landscaped gardens, swimming pools, private gyms and cinema rooms. It was 10 miles from our estate, just 10 miles. But really, it felt like another planet.

"I can see why Yousef likes coming here," I said to Mazen, still unable to speak about him in the past tense. "This is like Hollywood."

We turned into Gorse Bank Road, Hale, where Yousef had died, and my breath snagged in my throat. It was a wide, tree-lined avenue and − here it hit me like a sledge-hammer − it looked so safe. I couldn't begin to imagine a boy, my own brother, dying on this same stretch. It looked like the kind of neighbourhood where you would never find a scrap of litter, never mind a dying boy. The juxtaposition of what this place was, alongside what it had witnessed, was jaw-dropping. There was still police tape and a white tent around the spot where Yousef had been stabbed and as we passed, I wanted so much to feel something; a sign from him, a connection, a message even. But there was nothing. There were tributes and flowers pinned to the tree nearest to where he had died, but we didn't stop to read them. I was afraid of someone trying to speak to me, to offer condolences. I just wasn't strong enough. I had come to find the guard, and that was my focus. Our plan was to search for the security company where the guard worked, but before that, we spotted a guard, further up the street.

"Excuse me, I'm looking for a security guard called Paul," Mazen said, slowing the car down and opening his window.

"That's me," the man replied.

We explained who we were, and his face softened instantly with compassion. He told us that yes, he had been with Yousef during his final moments.

"I just tried to keep him talking and keep him distracted from what was happening," he said. "He couldn't reply, but I asked him to blink once for yes, twice for no, and I was asking him if he lived nearby and if he wanted me to do anything.

"I'm so sorry."

It was a comfort to know that Yousef hadn't been on his own, in those last minutes, and that he had seen a kind face, and heard words of reassurance, as he lost consciousness.

"Thank you," I whispered, blinded by tears.

Another guard, James, had seen an earlier disturbance between two boys. He told us too that a surgeon had come out of his home nearby, to try to save Yousef. But he was unsuccessful. The irony was unbearably painful. It had been Yousef's ambition to become a heart surgeon and buy himself one of these fancy houses. Instead, he had died on the street outside a surgeon's home.

I wasn't sorry to leave the big houses and the swanky cars behind. It wasn't their fault, I knew that. The vast majority of these people were doubtless law-abiding and decent. I'd heard first-hand accounts of kind and gentle souls who had tried in vain to save Yousef. But the whole image of this place suddenly seemed to me to be something of a sham. Behind the façade of respectability, and the influence and power which came with such mind-boggling wealth, there was a dark and twisted underbelly, an under-current of brutality and violence. Mum had believed – and me too – that mixing in this sort of environment would protect Yousef's future, not take it away. But as we drove

back, past the tree and the police tape and the tent, I felt
an inexplicable pull of longing and loss. I felt as though I
was leaving Yousef behind on that street, as though he would
want me to stay here, with him, with his spirit. There was
a gaping chasm of grief inside me, and it was threatening
to swallow me whole. When we arrived home, I spent a few
minutes in the car, to gather my thoughts, before putting on
a good mood for the children who were inside the house with
Maz and Mum.

"Your place is here, with us, Yousef," I whispered.
"This is your home."

It was a place he had dreamed of escaping. But now it
would always be his home. And he would forever be a boy
with a dream.

We were anxious to arrange Yousef's funeral as soon
as possible. As Muslims, we believed that Yousef should be
buried quickly, out of respect for him. Though Yousef wasn't
a devout Muslim, he attended prayers sometimes, either at
school or at the mosque. I'd actually taught him how to pray
myself years earlier, and I'd bought him a prayer mat too.
Of course, we'd never really talked about death with him,
at 17, that seemed many light years away. But he had once
mentioned, in a conversation with Mum, that he would like
a Muslim funeral and so we wanted to honour his wishes.

The post-mortem for the prosecution was completed in
that first week, and we hoped we could bury Yousef afterwards. But then, the defence counsel requested their own
post-mortem.

"Why can't they just use one pathologist, and one

post-mortem?" Mum wept. "It's so cruel. I can't bear to think of them cutting him up all over again."

But we were fast learning that, as the family of the victim, our thoughts and wishes mattered very little, in the justice process.

And Yousef seemed to not figure at all.

18

Eight days after Yousef's death, I went into MGS to thank the staff and students for their kind messages and flowers. We had been showered with cards and gifts and we were amazed and strengthened by the love they clearly had for him. Inside the entrance hall was a shrine of flowers, photos and letters, and it stopped me in my tracks. Many schools, especially one so prestigious and in the public eye, might have tried to brush this tragedy under the carpet, to distance themselves from an association with knife crime. But from that first day, MGS faced the grotesque reality head on and offered us whatever support and help they could. I read letters from pupils all across the school who wanted to share their memory of Yousef.

'You will never know how much you meant to us.'

'I will miss you, such a nice person with such a soft heart. Much love, brother.'

'I remember the first day in year 7 when we both knew no-one, we were in the same form and you were my first friend.'

'My best mate, the king, the funniest guy I've ever met, hope you're living on the other side, you were the softest guy ever...'

Young Yousef: An early family snap *(top)* of me and the baby brother I loved. *(Above)* smiling for the camera with Yousef when he was two years old

Together: Holding Yousef, aged three, during a stay in a homeless hostel

Beside the seaside: Enjoying a trip to Blackpool with Yousef in later years

Proud day: *(Above)* with mum Debbie and Yousef after winning a scholarship to Manchester Grammar School

Two of a kind: Mum worked long hours and sacrificed so much to look after us

Special bond: Yousef happily posing for a selfie with Mum

All smiles: Yousef laughing in school as he is caught on camera

On trial: Joshua Molnar fatally stabbed Yousef with a flick-knife but was cleared of murder and manslaughter

Two worlds: Adam Chowdhary *(pictured left, with Yousef right)* came from a very wealthy Cheshire family

Family outing: *(From left)* Yousef, me, Mazen, Raafat and Mum

Standing together: *(From left)* Mazen, me, Mum, sister Rachel, Raafat and Mazen on an evening out

'Justice for my uncle!': I was so proud when Raafat took the megaphone and spoke to the crowd at a protest. Yousef's father Ghaleb *(far left)* looks on

People power: Family, friends and supporters make their feelings known outside the Crown Court in Manchester

The painful truth: So many lives have been destroyed by knife crime. We need to show young people Yousef's blood-stained clothes and de-glamourise the myth. *(Top left)* the coat had a slash in it where Yousef was stabbed

'You were a strong fighter in the ring and a stronger person outside the ring. Your strength will continue to move us. Rest up champ.'

The words of these children, themselves shattered by Yousef's death, brought me comfort and sadness in equal measure. He had touched so many lives, but now he was gone. There was so much Yousef could have done, he had so much more to give. It turned out too that Yousef had often stayed behind after lessons to help the younger ones with their work.

'He told us never to tell anyone,' they confided. 'Or it would ruin his street cred!'

I smiled; that sounded like him. These were revelations; things we didn't know about Yousef, and it was a comfort to hear it from another perspective. On my way out of the school, Yousef's Chemistry teacher came to me and said:

"As Yousef was leaving school on the Thursday evening, before his death, he came running to me in the staff car park and tapped on my car window, because he was so determined to find out his latest exam result.

"I was going to tell him he had to wait until class on Monday but when I saw his face, I didn't have the heart. So I told him he had an A-star and he whooped and ran off down the pavement, celebrating.

"Of course, I never saw him again after that."

We both began to cry. It was just a small detail but in the context of his death, it was so important. I was grateful beyond words to the teacher for bending her rules and giving him the result earlier than planned. Because for Yousef, Monday never came.

Another of his friends from our estate came to see us that evening, to say Yousef had also helped to coach him through his GCSEs. I hadn't even known. But hearing all these voices, speaking so warmly about him, provided some solace and light in those dark hours.

Yousef's funeral was finally held 10 days after his death. It was tradition for men only to go to the service, but I went along with Maz and Raafat. Yousef's coffin would be open at the service, a prospect which understandably distressed Mum, and so she stayed at home with plans to come to the burial at the cemetery afterwards. She was so deeply traumatised that she was still hardly able to move out of her chair. She couldn't bring herself to even go upstairs, because she had to walk past Yousef's room. I went up to her bedroom each morning to bring down her clothes and at night, instead of sleeping in her own bed, she dozed on the sofa. She was barely sleeping or eating, and neither was I. Worse, we could see no end to it. Yet neither did we want an end to it.

"I don't want this pain to stop," Mum told me. "I want to feel his loss for the rest of his life. I'm his mother."

During the night, when she occasionally slept, I'd hear her shouting Yousef's name. Sometimes she woke up screaming. Other times, she was sobbing. I held her like a child, with my arms tight around her, the way I had once held Yousef.

On the morning of the funeral, I found a black dress in the wardrobe for Mum to wear and carried it downstairs. Outside the Dar Al Hadi Foundation in Ardwick, it was bleak and raining. The Manchester palette offered an array of mournful and desolate greys.

"Is Yousef crying because he is sad?" Raafat asked me. "Is that why it's raining?"

I shook my head and forced a smile.

"Yousef is happy in heaven," I said, but I felt wretched as I spoke. I wished I could truly believe that.

Yousef's friends all gathered around the entrance in black suits, heads bowed, tears streaming. MGS had chartered buses to bring children to the service. One of Yousef's close friends bravely stepped forwards, in the rain, to make a statement to the waiting reporters:

"He was the son every parent dreams of: loving, caring, kind, yet ambitious and determined. We have no doubt he would have lived to fulfil his dream of becoming a heart surgeon. Instead he was taken away from us as a result of a stab wound to his heart.

"Yousef's life will not have been taken in vain if we are able to achieve something positive from the debate that has ensued following his death.

"More police officers on the streets to help protect our young people may be a good start. We will miss Yousef so dearly. May he rest in peace."

Inside the mosque, Yousef's body lay in an open coffin in the middle of the room. This was my chance to say goodbye to him; my chance to represent Mum. But the knowledge that Yousef was lying quietly just metres away whilst people milled around him seemed both disturbing and absurd. *'Check my hair! Is my hair OK? All these people! I don't even have a mirror!'*

I would have crumbled completely if I'd been on my own,

but I had to stay strong for the two boys. There were prayers and recitals and so many tears. After the service, Yousef's body was driven past MGS and also Ladybarn, his primary school. Though the schools had closed for the day, there were hundreds of children outside each one, paying their respects. The sight of so many young people weeping left me with a feeling of overwhelming hopelessness. I thought of how we had scrimped and saved to make the sacrifices to send Yousef to a grammar school; to help him break away from the area where we lived. And yet, it was through those very connections at the school that he had died. I thought about the leafy, wealthy Cheshire suburbs, favoured by footballers from Manchester United and Manchester City and stars of film and TV, the places where Mum had encouraged him to hang out, believing he would be safe. Yet he had bled to death on one of those same streets. Perhaps the cruellest irony was Yousef's ambition to become a heart surgeon, but he had died from a stab wound to the heart.

His death had devastated hundreds upon hundreds of young people; I saw them now as we drove slowly past; young faces, grief-stricken, confused and angry. Yousef's death had reverberated throughout the entire city like a tuning fork; the effects felt far and wide and so deep.

At Manchester's Southern Cemetery, we met up with Mum, who looked almost see-through, she was so pale. All the colour and depth had been washed out of her and I had a sudden flash of panic that she might well disappear altogether. Yousef was to be buried in the Islamic section. It was still raining and cold, gloomy and dismal, and there was a biting and unforgiving wind. But as Yousef's body was lowered into the grave, there was a glimmer of sunshine, piercing through the clouds. I fancied it might be one of Yousef's long, slim hands, reaching down to us, from heaven. *'I'm here, sis, I'm here.'*

After the burial, there was no wake or gathering to commemorate his life. We were all far too upset, weighted with sadness and exhaustion. We could not pretend otherwise. Maz and Raafat had found the funeral service, with the open coffin, macabre and gruesome and, as we left the cemetery, they were my only concern.

"I wish I hadn't gone," Raafat told me. "I wanted to remember Uncle Yo-Yo playing basketball and teaching me algebra. Not like this."

On our way home from the service, I stopped at Domino's to treat him to his favourite pizza, a cheese and tomato special. We went home to watch a film and play with the children. I knew that Yousef, wherever he was, would approve of that.

19

Yousef's funeral brought no closure for us, and even though I had seen his body lowered into the ground myself, I still listened out for the sound of his key in the door, for the soft sound of him dumping his school bag and kicking off his school shoes in the hallway, and the familiar and well-rehearsed: *'Mum! I'm starving!'*

When I was washing the dishes, I'd see his ghostly outline messing around in the back garden, playing basketball, or shadow boxing with his nephews. Sometimes, it was so clear, it was like a hallucination. Rachel and I were so worried about Mum that we had arranged for her to stay in a hotel for a night after the funeral, to get her out of the house and away from the reporters. And afterwards, Rachel suggested taking her to Devon for a week, to allow her to get over the trauma of the burial a little, in a place where nobody knew who she was. We understood that everyone had the best intentions, but it was just too much for her to be constantly bombarded with visitors and messages and calls. Before Mum went to Devon, I packed a case for her and upstairs, on the landing, I felt myself drawn towards Yousef's bedroom. The door was slightly ajar, as Mum had insisted. It was funny, because usually he insisted on having it tightly closed: *'I'm 17! I need my privacy!'*

At night, he would open it a little, so that he had the light from the landing. Even at 17, he wasn't completely comfortable in the dark. Thinking of him alone in the dark now, in the cemetery, tore me apart. In those days after the funeral, I remembered out of the blue that my own email address was the recovery email for Yousef's social media pages, since I had been the one to set them up for him when he was a young teenager. And so I would now be able to access his accounts.

"I can look on his Snapchat and his Instagram," I said to Caroline, the liaison officer.

She agreed it would be really helpful to the investigation. Frustratingly, the police had no access to Yousef's phone itself, because we didn't know his passcode. I couldn't believe that the phone companies weren't legally obliged to help, even in a murder investigation. But it made my own research all the more important. I began trawling through his Instagram and WhatsApp pages, looking for information and passing on everything I found to the police. On Snapchat, my blood suddenly froze in my veins as I came across a short video showing a knife, sent from Adam's account to Yousef, just three days before he was killed.

"Look at this!" I said to Mazen. "Why on earth would Adam send Yousef a video of a knife?"

It sent a chill through me.

But I wanted the truth, at all costs, and I forwarded it straight to the police. Could this have been the same knife which pierced his heart? It was unthinkable.

There was an exchange too between the two boys

where Yousef threatened to stab Adam and he replied: "Do it man" with a laughing emoji. It was hard, given our tragedy, to see such an offensive comment in context; total nonsense between two immature, silly teenagers, complete with light-hearted emojis. But again, despite the possible repercussions for the prosecution and defence, I sent it to the police. The video of the knife, of course, was far from nonsensical. And interspersed with those disturbing messages between the boys were mundane questions about their biology homework and back and forth discussions about which pizza place they might prefer on a Friday night. One voice note from Yousef, just four days before his death, said:

'Bro I'm joking I'm going to do an all nighter, I'm going to have bare (lots of) coffee and stay up I ain't failing these tests bro you mad? I got big plans, big money you get me. What's one night fam come on. Bio (logy) is a sticky one but i cant f**k up all of them bro, I need to do something innit.'

"Why is he speaking like that?" I asked, puzzled.

He certainly didn't talk like that at home.

"All teenage lads speak like that," Mazen reassured me. "It's just a phase. They do it to impress their mates, trying to look cool. He would have grown out of it, if he'd had the chance."

He was right. And more than anything, Yousef's enthusiasm and his desire to do well shone through in that message. Yousef's idea of drastic action was to stay up all night drinking coffee! He was not a gangster or a hardman. These innocent exchanges jarred so sharply with the footage of the knife. There were thousands upon thousands of messages, mostly all completely harmless, often moaning about extra chores, strict parents, too much homework. Above all, this was a reminder that they were children.

And that Yousef would eternally remain so.

As I trawled for evidence, the photos and videos of Yousef were balm to my wounded soul; they were my way of connecting with him, of keeping his memory alive. What I loved most on his accounts were the funny little video clips; Yousef boxing in the back garden with Raafat, Yousef teaching Raafat to play ukulele, Yousef and Maz cheering as they watched a football match on TV. There was even a years-old clip of the boys' magic show; wowing Mum with the disappearing coin trick. I laughed all over again when I watched it. They were small, seemingly inconsequential moments; mundane and every-day, but now, they were all I had left. I felt myself magnetically drawn to the clips, watching them over and over, finding vicarious comfort through the two-dimensional world of social media, but it was comfort all the same.

But Mum was different. Even after she came home from Devon, she was unable to return to the house; it held too many memories, too many nightmares.

"I can't go back in there," she told me sadly. "I can't do it. I see him in every room, and it breaks my heart."

Though she and I were similar in many ways, we dealt with our grief from opposite standpoints. Unlike me, she didn't want to see pictures of Yousef or memories of him on Facebook, and she couldn't bear to hear updates from the police. She couldn't cope with the brutality of the situation which had been slammed upon her. For Mum, I think, any acknowledgement of her loss risked unleashing a giant dam of grief and once it rushed out, she would never be able to divert it back. Yet these snippets of reminiscence, these tenuous links with Yousef, were what kept me going and kept my head above the water. But they were pushing Mum deeper under the surface, so that she had to fight for breath. I could see she was flailing; she was drowning. She blamed herself, too, for being too soft and allowing Yousef to meet with his friends that Friday evening after his day off school.

"If I'd stood my ground, and kept him at home, he might still be alive," she said, wringing her hands in self-reproach.

She was not responsible, and deep down, I hope she knew that. But as a mother your first job is to keep your child safe, and she tortured herself over and over that she had failed Yousef. I, too, chided myself. Why hadn't I stepped in, and stopped him from leaving the house? Why hadn't I looked more closely at his 'friends?' The guilt swilled round and round in my mind like sewage; toxic and infected. There were moments too, especially at night, when the dark silence was swollen with recrimination even towards Yousef.

"Why did you leave us?" I asked him angrily, the question burning my throat. "Why?"

It was an outlet for my frustration, nothing more, and as dawn came, I took a firm hold of my thoughts once again. This wasn't Yousef's fault, or mine, or Mum's.

We applied to the council for emergency help and Mum and Maz were given a new flat, in Chorlton, a short distance across the city. The family home was to remain empty, for now. The council agreed to give Mum four months to decide what she wanted to do, for her and Maz's future. But though she couldn't live in the house, Mum couldn't bear the thought of strangers in there either; a new boy in Yousef's room, a new crowd playing footy in the back garden; a new family redecorating the house, papering over the past, wiping out his existence.

"Why don't I apply to take over the tenancy?" I suggested. "Mazen and I could move in there, with our three boys. That way, you and Maz can visit, when you feel up to it."

It was a bold idea. Truth was, I was just so desperate to keep hold of the house and to keep hold of Yousef. I made an application and crossed my fingers.

"Wish me luck, Yousef," I whispered.

Even though the house was now empty, I still had to pass the front door four times a day, there and back on the school runs. And one morning, after dropping Raafat at the school gates, my footsteps took me up the familiar path, almost against my will, and before I knew it, I was turning my key in the lock. I slipped in through the front door without thinking, as I had done thousands of times before.

"Just for a few moments," I told myself.

It was as though I couldn't help myself. Walking inside, I was struck at once by the yawning emptiness. The hallway ached with loneliness. The silence stretched and gaped like an open wound. This was once a house filled with laughter, bickering and chaos. Normally, I'd be falling over a pile of school shoes, trainers, and football boots in the doorway. There'd be a backpack, maybe even a coat, lying on the floor. Upstairs, probably rap music blaring and the faint scent of Lynx and unwashed socks wafting down the stairs.

Now, I could see a fuzzy image of Mum, part way down the stairs, with an armful of dirty washing:

'Turn that racket down boys! I can't hear myself think!'

And there was Maz, peering over the banister, headphones around his neck, his trademark shy smile. And then Yousef, beautiful, bright Yousef, shadow-boxing his way along the landing and bounding down the stairs, two at a time, eyes shining, arms outstretched, beaming. Yes, really beaming.

'Here's my lovely sister!'

My heart leapt in my chest, and I reached out to him with already redundant arms. The picture was quickly fading out of focus, and it began to disintegrate. He wasn't here. He would never be here again. In the living room, I sank to the floor, with my arms huddled around my knees. The walls; once filled with pictures and family photos, were now empty; bleachy and jaundiced. I watched silently as a treasured montage of the dramas from years gone by played out in my mind: Little Yousef reading medical books at the dining table, his short, chubby fingers tracing each word. Teenage Yousef celebrating his exam results, dancing round the room. Outside in the garden was a solitary football and a forgotten skipping rope. The basketball hoop seemed to sulk at me, sullen, brooding, as though it was put out by the inactivity. I could almost hear the sound of Yousef's trainers rhythmically tapping the flagstones as he skipped:

'*Ninety-eight, ninety-nine, one hundred!*'

My boys were always so impressed by the way he skipped, and they loved to watch him; either on tiptoes inside, through the living window or outside, sitting on the doorstep, counting his reps for him. Sometimes, amongst the chaos of the house, I used to long for a bit of peace; those moments of silence were like a welcome sigh of relief. Now, I longed instead for the noise; the arguments, the giggling, the bad language floating down from the bedrooms. '*Only banter, Mum!*'

Upstairs, Yousef's bedroom was still untouched. I tiptoed in, for some reason fearful of making a noise, as though he was perhaps sleeping underneath his duvet, and I might disturb him. I threw myself onto the crumpled bed and buried my face in his pillow. There was a faint scent of him, still; aftershave and shampoo, mingled with stale sweat. He felt so near to me, so near as I drank in those familiar smells. Yet I knew, the moment I raised my head, he would drift far, far again – and out of reach. Inside his wardrobe, there were rows and rows of his clothes. I spotted his favourite football shirt; a green Germany top from World Cup 2018. His Manchester United shirt was there too. He'd been to one game at Old Trafford, years earlier, thanks to tickets donated by a friend, and I was so thankful, thinking of that now. We'd had no idea his time would be so short. I found his prom suit on another hanger and remembered how proud we had been, how full of hope for his future.

Rummaging in the bottom of the wardrobe, I heard a clinking sound and to my surprise I pulled out four or five empty bottles of lager. Honestly! That was typical of Yousef. He and his friends had no doubt shared a couple of secret beers and instead of throwing them away, he had simply stashed them in his wardrobe, out of sight, out of mind.

'I forgot about those! I was going to get rid of them when Mum wasn't looking. Honest!'

"You're so lazy," I chided him.

And despite myself, I laughed. Yousef could still make me smile, even now, across the divide. Leaving the house, I felt lighter, stronger somehow. And in those dark days that followed, visiting the house became my catharsis. It was like a fix, a pull so strong that I could not have ignored it even if I had wanted to. As it was, I really looked forward to it.

Each time, I'd go into Yousef's room, sit on his bed, close my eyes, and make-believe. This was my time with him, my counselling, my therapy. In the house, the smells, the tastes, the memories, all flooded back. I loved watching them playing on an imaginary film reel in my mind; the chronicles of a life well lived and lost. It was an exquisite and addictive pain. Here he was, on a donkey, on our first trip to Blackpool. And what about the time he and Maz piled their plates so high in the all-you-can-eat-buffet that the other diners started laughing at them? And Yousef dancing around the kitchen, twirling Mum around, to the sounds of '70s disco classics. What I would have given for just one moment back with him, for just one more chance to tell him how much he was loved. Because he was loved. *'I know that you silly thing. I always knew that.'*

On one visit at the house, racked with sobs and with my whole heart raging against it, I reluctantly began packing away his things. It was a job which had to be done, and it had been pressing heavily on me for weeks now.

"Sorry Yo-Yo," I whispered. "I have to do this. I want you to know I'm throwing nothing away. I'm saving everything in the loft."

I soon regretted saying that, because in his drawers I came across empty bottles of aftershave. Behind the wardrobe were more discarded bottles of beer, chocolate wrappers, price tags from new clothes.

"Yousef!" I exclaimed. "Ever heard of a bin?"

His desk was a messy pile of calculators, books, pens, and rulers, mixed in with hair gel, aftershaves and deodorants. There was even a stray bag of chilli flavoured crisps nestling in there too; one of his favourite snacks. In a drawer, I found his 16th birthday card from Mum.

'I love you very much, my beautiful boy,' she had written.

"Me too," I whispered. "Me too."

20

In April, just over a month after Yousef's death, the High Master from Manchester Grammar School contacted us to ask if we would like to attend a memorial service for Yousef. Though so soon after his passing, the staff felt that a day of remembrance and celebration might help many of their pupils who were grieving, and us too, of course.

"Yes, absolutely," I said. "We'd love to come, thank you."

It was difficult for Mum, she had to work up to the challenge of just leaving the flat, and then of facing lots of people who would want to talk about Yousef and reminisce.

"I will be with you," I assured her. "You won't be on your own."

For me, it was a day to look forward to. I loved hearing about Yousef, seeing his photos, watching his video clips. It was like a quasi-resurrection, the closest I would come to ever seeing him for real again. We were told that all the flowers brought into school after Yousef's death would be used as compost for a memorial tree, to be planted in the school grounds.

"The tree will last forever," I told the boys, as we got ready for the service. "It will live longer than all of us."

On the tree would be a plaque with Yousef's name and dates of birth and death. It was a lovely idea; sensitive and well thought out, and typical of the teachers at MGS. At the tree planting, there was a balloon release planned, with red balloons, Yousef's favourite colour. *'Manchester United! Good choice!'*

It was an overcast Saturday morning but there were still several hundred guests there. After a two-minute silence, the balloons were released into the air. Then, as they floated into the distance, the first drops of rain began to fall, quickly they grew quite heavy, and there was a change of plan. We were all directed inside, to the great hall, ready for the speeches. My heart dropped like a stone. I wasn't sure I could cope with being back inside the hall again. Suddenly, in a whoosh, I was back in September 2013, for Yousef's first day at MGS. I could see him sitting on the stage, the bright eyes, the cheeky wave. And then in my mind's eye I could see him too as he walked down the corridor, away from me and out of reach. I remembered the irrational panic I felt; would he be swallowed up by this place, would we lose him?

Yes, we would.

My legs were like jelly as we walked into the building. I desperately didn't want to go into the hall, but I could see no way of avoiding it either. I had to stay strong, for Mum, for Maz, for the kids. As we walked inside, one of the teachers said to me:

"Would you like to say a few words, Jade? It's entirely your choice."

"No, I'm sorry, I really can't," I replied, wobbly and on the edge of tears.

But then Raafat, who was holding my hand, piped up and said to the teacher: "I will say a few words instead."

He made me smile suddenly; he was only nine years old, but he had that same indefatigable confidence and buoyant self-belief, just like Yousef. And just as Yousef had calmed my nerves on that first day in the big hall, so Raafat did now.

First, there were speeches from Yousef's friends, including Yas, and some of Yousef's teachers. The ceremony was interspersed with video clips and photographs from his life, as well as his favourite music. And then, without a single show of nerves, Raafat walked proudly onto the stage, and said:

"Thank you for this memorial to my Uncle Yousef. We miss him very much."

His speech was short and cute, and it brought the house down; there was clapping and crying all around me. As we walked back outside, down gloomy corridors and past empty classrooms, I fancied I could see Yousef sitting at a desk, head bowed, pen in hand, forehead creased in concentration, pushing his glasses onto his nose the way he did when he was thinking hard. Outside, on the damp sports fields, I strained to hear his voice: *'Pass! Pass, I'm onside!'* He was here, at MGS, in the classrooms, and on the pitches. His memory lived on.

The memorial service was reported in the local newspaper and the High Master at MGS, Dr Martin Boulton, said: "Yousef was a dearly loved young man, and an incredibly bright pupil.

"The memorial service was about paying tribute to Yousef and remembering all that he had achieved in his life. It was so moving to hear from his family and his closest friends – the people knew him best – about what a caring young man he was, who would have done anything for his friends and family and touched so many people's lives."

He had loved it there, there was no doubt about that. And yet, at MGS, he had met Adam Chowdhary. And during that time, Joshua Molnar had emerged on the scene too.

21

Mazen had requested a succession of meetings with the police, three in total, to keep us up to date with how the case was progressing, although we knew nothing more about the evidence against the two defendants. I was still speaking to our family liaison officer a couple of times a week too. Now that the evidence gathering was complete, and they had all the information they needed from us, they had become far more sympathetic and helpful. I had at times felt a little intimidated or indignant at their questions, but now I realised that it was a necessary process, that these were all steps along the road to justice. And as a result, our relationship became much more positive; we became good friends. With Kath, especially, I developed a close bond which I knew would last way beyond the criminal proceedings.

Mazen and I also met with Jane, one of the paramedics who had been called to attend to Yousef shortly after he was stabbed. The moment I saw her, I felt soothed; she had a compassionate, gentle face and a maternal manner. I said to her:

"I waited years for my brother. I longed for him. And when he was born, I felt like I'd won every lottery there ever was. Yet all it took was one stab wound, one knife, to take him away from me."

Jane did not speak but she wrapped her arms around me, her eyes bright with tears. Though the encounter was intense, it was also cathartic. If there was any solace to be found in Yousef's passing, it was in meeting people like Kath and Jane; total strangers who had offered themselves to us at our most painful and intimate moments. Jane even drew a picture for us, which symbolised Yousef's final moments, and I hung it in the kitchen. These little kindnesses helped to deflate a little of the pressure around us. Ultimately, for me, it was the children once again who kept me going; they were my comfort and my crutch. We had to get through each day, with smiles, with normality, for their sakes. Like most mums, my days were organised with a military precision; breakfast, school run, house-work, toddler group, school run, homework, bath and bed. I needed to be rushed off my feet and thankfully, I was. For Mum, it wasn't so straightforward; she was reminded constantly and cruelly of how her daily tasks had been sliced in two; only one son left to cook for, to clean for, to wash for. Only one son left to love. I watched her, day by day, sinking deeper into a quicksand of despair, yet I could not pull her out, for I was in danger of sinking myself.

For me, the night times were the worst, when the children were all tucked up in bed, and the house was quiet. I hated having time to think. Mazen and I both tried to be strong, for each other, and sometimes, that meant staying silent. In the early hours, when the house was quiet,

I'd find myself standing at the window, staring out across the street, across the city and beyond.

"Where are you, Yousef?" I whispered.

Still, a tiny part of me thought I might be able to somehow connect with him. I held onto a crazy notion that I might be able to reach him, on the other side, and that my love alone might be strong enough to resurrect him and bring him home. I thought back to my trip to the hospital, as a little girl, Mum beaming in the hospital bed, Yousef in a cot at the side.

'Is he ours? Is he really ours?'

I remembered the way I'd hopped from one foot to the other, hardly able to believe my luck. Oh, how I had loved him; my new baby brother. Surely a bond like that didn't just dissolve and disappear? There had to be a way I could find him and bring him back. Hour after hour, I stood at the window, huge swathes of love and longing stretching out, into the darkness, like tendrils, ready to seek him out. I could feel the love, diffusing physically from my core, out of the window and across the city. A misty shroud of belonging. A warm cloak around Yousef, to carry him home.

"Where are you?" I whispered again. "Send me a sign."

If I slept at all, it was only in fits and starts. I dreaded going to sleep because I knew that, waking up, I'd have to face reality again. I suffered with a recurring nightmare too, which spooked me, every single time. In it, Yousef was sitting opposite me, looking straight at me with his usual cheeky grin. I could even see the crinkles around his eyes when he smiled. I remembered the way he pushed his glasses up his nose. He was so real – he was so *there* – that even in the dream, I found it hard to recognise that this was only a dream.

"People keep telling me that you're dead and I can't accept it," I told him. "I won't have it."

I waited for him to reply, but he just didn't speak.

"Yousef!" I prompted him. "Tell me that you're alive. Tell me it didn't happen."

But still, he grinned, and still, he remained silent. Frustrated, and becoming scared, I leaned over to shake him by the shoulder.

"Yousef!" I said again. "Stop messing about now. You're scaring me."

And it was then, in a flash of blinding white horror, that I realised that he was wearing the same outfit in which he had died; that black coat, the grey cargo pants, his pristine white trainers. And seeping out from underneath the jacket, dark and sticky across my hands, was the blood from his wound. It spattered over his trainers in thick clots.

And yet still he smiled and still he did not speak.

Always at this point, I woke up, gasping for breath, my heart pounding as I flicked on the bedside light to check that my hands were not dripping with blood. I had that same nightmare hundreds of times, night after night after night. I became too afraid to sleep, dreading going to bed because of the terrors it brought. This technicoloured terror ran through my mind on a relentless, punishing circuit. It was more exhausting going to bed than staying up all night. I would sit, bolt upright against my pillows, watching the clock tick round, so slowly, waiting for one of the boys to wake and shout my name.

"Mummy! Mummy!"

The morning brought glorious and welcome relief, because it signalled the end of my thinking time. But the children missed him too; their grief a mixture of confusion, sadness and annoyance.

"Where is he?" two-year-old Zack asked crossly, toddling from room to room. "Where is my Uncle Yo-Yo?"

Because Mum had moved to a new home, he thought that Yousef had somehow been left behind or he was perhaps playing a game of hide and seek which had long since lost its lustre. Or other times he would stand in the middle of the living room and shout Yousef's name at the top of his voice.

"I can see him," he told me. "I can see Uncle Yo-Yo over there, by the window."

We clung to the notion that Yousef's spirit might be visible to Zack, that there might even be some communication between them. They were mere wisps of hope; scraps of solace; as insubstantial as they were desperate. But they were all we had.

Raafat, nine, had looked up to Yousef, worshipped him, and they had done so much together. As well as tutoring him for grammar school, Yousef had taught him to box and play football. And not long before his death, he'd started teaching Raafat how to play badminton. Raafat had lost his uncle, his role-model, his hero. In the early days after we lost Yousef, Raafat made a little shrine at the side of Yousef's desk, with a light-up tree and a little letter 'Y' hanging from the branches. Mum allowed him, and only him, to go into the bedroom to be near to his beloved uncle. Sometimes, when I passed on the landing, I'd overhear Raafat talking to Yousef, chatting away, as though the two of them were sitting side by side.

"And I came top of the class in Science," I heard Raafat say. "I knew you'd be chuffed with that. I remembered what you told me about laying my facts down clearly."

Though Raafat understood more than the little ones about death, we hadn't yet told him about the way Yousef had died; it hadn't seemed appropriate or fair for his young age. But inevitably, his pals at school all talked about the tragedy. Yousef himself had attended the same school so he was known to many of the children and their older siblings, and of course all of the teachers. After hearing many different accounts about that evening, Raafat had decided to Google 'Yousef Makki' himself. One night, before bed, he asked me:

"Was Uncle Yo-Yo stabbed to death by his friend?"

I hesitated. I couldn't lie to him. But I couldn't tell him the truth either.

Raafat sensed the conflict in my eyes and said: "How could his friend do that to him? I don't understand."

"Me neither," I said softly.

I felt wretched that my young son had turned to the internet for information.

I blamed myself for not telling him the facts, and I felt guilty that my own grief was clouding the way that I coped with his.

"From now on, if you need to know anything, you must ask me," I said. "I will be completely open with you. I can't promise you the answers, there's a lot I don't know myself. But I will always tell you the truth."

Mazen, though he was the rock of our family, had moments of intense grief and despair. After Yousef's death he took a period of sickness from his work as a chemist, and afterwards decided on a change of career, working in residential homes with troubled children. He supported and mentored teenage boys who had become embroiled in gangs and county lines drugs operations.

"I want to understand what goes wrong with teenagers who turn to crime," he said. "If I can help to turn one life around, it might save a life. It might save someone else's son, someone else's brother."

Maz, too, was struggling acutely with the loss of his brother. As little ones, he and Yousef had been inseparable; stuck together like glue. But like all teenage boys, they had bickered and fought, and their relationship was very much a work in progress when Yousef died. It was a first draft, full of mistakes. I have no doubt that, if Yousef had lived, they would have become best friends again after puberty. Now, that would never happen. Their love would never come full circle. Like all of us, Maz was eaten up with regret.

"Why didn't I lend him my T-shirt the weekend before he died?"

"Why didn't I have that game of FIFA with him?"

"Why did I never tell him I loved him?"

I hated to see him pull himself apart.

"Teenage brothers don't ever say they love each other," I said to Maz. "But he knew. Of course he knew."

It was seeing Maz in such distress that seemed to trigger a change in Mum. She vowed to introduce normality and functionality back into their lives and she made a huge effort to pull herself out of her depression.

"Maz needs me," she said. "I've got to do it, for him. I can't help Yousef now, but I have a son who needs me here and I have to focus on him."

I had so much admiration for her. This was the Mum I knew and loved; capable, loving and selfless. She started getting dressed and cooking and washing and shopping again. She cooked Maz's favourite spicy chicken and took him out for treats. They went to the cinema for a singalong for 'The Greatest Showman' and when they came home, Maz was rolling his eyes and laughing in mock embarrassment.

"Honestly, Mum was the only one singing!" he told me. "And she was so loud!"

It was lovely to see him so cheerful, to see him step out of the shade, even if only for a moment. He and Mum visited Yousef's grave most days too. Mum still found it almost impossible to talk about Yousef, but little by little, she was taking small steps through the smog of her own sadness, so that she could help to guide Maz through his.

In May 2019, I took the plunge and had a tattoo of Yousef's initials on my arm. I wasn't a big fan of tattoos, not for myself, but I wanted a lasting reminder, on the outside, not just in my head. I chose a small and simple design, Yousef's initials with a picture of a crown on the top, because of course, as a baby, he had been our king. He would always be our king. In the days afterwards, many of Yousef's friends had the same image done. The tattoo represented, and I can see it now, another attempt to stay close to Yousef, another way of keeping him alive. It was another defence mechanism, to keep me upright and stop me from spilling over. It was false hope. It was cruel deception. I knew, in the depths of my soul, that I had to let him go, but I simply could not.

22

Early in June 2019, Yousef's boxing gym hosted a charity night in his memory. Mazen's friend, Riz Khan, was behind the initiative, working hard to gather sponsors. And Omar, the boxing coach, who had kindly driven Yousef home from his last boxing session just 48 hours before his death, offered his expertise too. "We want to do something, we feel so helpless," he told us. "We want his name to live on, here in the gym."

The plan was to launch a bursary fund in Yousef's name for children who could not afford the £2 training sessions. There were, I knew, many children like that, certainly in our neighbourhood. And there were many children also whose lives would be dramatically transformed by spending time in a gym, far away from the all too tempting lure of drugs, alcohol and violent crime.

The boxers Amir Khan and Tyson Fury sent memorabilia to be auctioned. There were amateur boxing fights scheduled too throughout the evening. We all went, as a family, to the charity evening. All, that is, except Yousef. It felt so odd, walking into his boxing gym, meeting his sparring partners and his coaches, and yet he wasn't there. I imagined how proud he would have been to show us around: *'Look, here's the boxing bag, and here's the ring. This is where I skip. This is where I get a shower. Come on Raafat, put these gloves on and show me your best hook.'*

The evening raised an amazing £13, 000 for the boxing bursary. "That's a lot of training sessions for a lot of kids," I smiled. "Yousef would be well pleased."

And afterwards, one of the gym rooms was renamed: 'The Yousef Makki Room.' It pulled at my heartstrings that Yousef had met so many kind and generous and wonderful people in his life. He loved them. And they all loved him back. Yet it took one bad apple. Just one.

To our surprise, the trial was listed for later in June 2019, a little over three months after Yousef's death. It was quick, we were told, for a murder trial, but the CPS assured us they had everything in place. We had no prior experience of court procedure and so we accepted everything that we were told. Besides, I had absolute confidence in the police, the SIO Colin Larkin, and the team of prosecution lawyers. I had complete faith that we would get justice for Yousef. Still now, all we knew was that Yousef had been stabbed with a knife, bought on the internet and that Joshua Molnar had admitted killing him, in self-defence or by accident only, on a smart street in Cheshire. From a certain perspective, I was anxious to get the trial underway. My mind was a whirl of questions, theories, and scenarios. I needed an explanation and I needed answers. More than anything, I needed justice. But at the same time, I was apprehensive and fearful, knowing I would have to face Yousef's former friends in court and hear the ghastly details of his death.

The week before the trial began, I found a day nursery for Zack and Daniel. I didn't like them being away from me and normally they were at home full-time. But I knew, for the next few weeks, I had to focus on Yousef. The next day, I went into Primark and bought myself a couple of cheap black outfits. It felt odd, tasteless even, buying new clothes for a murder trial. Usually I would only buy myself new clothes for a special birthday celebration or a holiday. But I was all too aware from the stories in the media that we were being portrayed as poor and disadvantaged, and that we were being pitted, rightly or wrongly, against the immense wealth and privilege of the defendants' families. I was determined then, to present myself well and to maintain my dignity and self-respect. Luckily, that didn't cost a thing. I didn't want to let Yousef down. *'Jade, just be yourself. That's enough for me.'*

The first day of the trial dawned warm and sunny and there was a feeling of expectation in the air; summer was here, and the schools would soon be breaking up for the long holidays. There was a general feeling of relief amongst the mums at the school gates and amidst our friends and neighbours.

"Not long now until we go to Spain! Can't wait for a lie-in when school finishes! Anyone fancy a trip to the coast?"

But for me, the arrival of summer signified only anxiety and trauma. For all I could think about, as the sun burst through the curtains, was my brother. That first morning, I was so tense and jittery that I couldn't even manage a cup of coffee, never mind think about breakfast.

"You must eat," Mazen urged me.

But he was the same. Neither of us had the stomach for cereal and I tipped both bowls into the recycling, untouched. We dropped the children at nursery and took Raafat to school, both trying to maintain an air of order and routine. The other mums saw my black outfit, my sombre expression, and squeezed my arm in solidarity. With the children safely delivered, we got the tram into the city centre, to Manchester Crown Court. I was already uptight and sweating and it was made worse because the weather was so hot. It was a minor inconvenience, but I was fretting about arriving in court with a shiny face and tell-tale sweat marks down my black blouse. These things didn't matter, I knew. But it was as if, by focussing on the minutiae, I could somehow avoid the screaming pain of my reality. I didn't want to think about the murder trial. I preferred to think about my mascara running in the heat.

We had arranged to meet Mum and Maz outside the court buildings, in Crown Square. Maz was taking time off school to attend the trial. Mum, like me, looked like a bag of nerves. The apprehension was scrawled right across her face. Her forehead was a concertina of wrinkles and there were etchings of sorrow across her cheeks. Each line, each mark told its own sad story. Yet despite it all, she was here, and she was here for Yousef. Loss had made Mum hard-wearing – but never hard. In spite of all her suffering, she had retained her tenderness, her dignity and her humour. She had high standards and they never dipped. Today, she was wearing a cross and chain, in Yousef's memory, and clutching his photograph in her hand.

"I didn't think he'd want to miss out," she said, nodding at the photo. "So I brought him along."

I knew she'd take strength from that.

"Let's get a coffee," Mazen suggested. "We're a little early."

But my hands were trembling so much that I dropped my cup and spilled the scalding liquid all down my new Primark blouse. I was so annoyed with myself; I'd bought new clothes to try to make a good impression, to show what a decent, caring family Yousef had. Now I was covered in stains!

"Look, don't panic," Mazen said calmly. "Primark is just over there. You've plenty of time to run in, choose a new shirt, and get changed."

I was so thankful that one of us at least was thinking clearly. Outside the court we met up with Ghaleb and some of Yousef's friends and teachers from MGS. Yas was there along with a clutch of other boys, and the teachers had drawn up a rota so that someone from the school would be here to represent them each day. They even had a staff member taking notes, to report back to everyone else. It was heart-warming, even under such stress, to know that Yousef's teachers had cared so much about him; they still treated him as though he was one of their own. It was a boost to have so many familiar faces around us, but still, the tension buzzed through me. *'You'll be fine, sis. Just don't spill any more coffee!'*

The court room itself, Court Two, was daunting; old-fashioned with high ceilings, ornate plasterwork and dark mahogany benches. This was my first time ever inside a court, and the same for Mum, Mazen and Maz too. It was frightening for us, overwhelming, even though we had done nothing wrong. I'd been told that the defendants and their families had been given a tour around the court, prior to the case, so that they could familiarise themselves with the environment. We, as the victim's family, hadn't been offered the same service. Perhaps that early omission ought to have been a warning bell for me but naively, I didn't hear it. I had full trust in the British justice system.

We saw the family of each defendant, as we were taking our seats, but I made no eye contact, no communication. They had their own trauma, I recognised that, and I was respectful of it, as I always had been. But there was no room in my head for compassion or sympathy. No room for anyone else but Yousef.

I listened as the legal teams were introduced. Mr Johnson and Miss Crangle appeared on behalf of the prosecution. Mr Webster QC and Mr Leach QC represented Joshua Molnar. Miss Laws QC and Mr Corsellis QC appeared on behalf of Adam Chowdhary.

That first day was taken up with introductions, and then with legal argument and discussion. The language and terminology were baffling, and I had to concentrate hard to follow everything. Despite applications from the press, the two boys, both aged 17 but close to 18, could not be publicly named. Joshua Molnar was referred to as Boy One. Adam Chowdhary was referred to as Boy Two.

Then the judge agreed to move the trial to Court Three which was apparently lighter and more modern, after complaints that Court Two was 'Dickensian' and not appropriate for juvenile defendants. In the new court, the press members were told they were not allowed in the courtroom itself because of a lack of seats and they were sent to the public gallery. There were more complaints about that.

It seemed to me as though everyone was having their say; the defendants, the press, the legal teams. But not us. Never us. Again, trusting and artless, I accepted that.

Before the jury was sworn in, the defendants entered pleas to the charges. Joshua Molnar, dressed in a smart, expensive-looking suit, pleaded not guilty to murder but admitted perverting the course of justice. He pleaded guilty to possessing a flick knife. Boy Two admitted possessing a flick knife but denied perverting the course of justice. Both denied conspiracy to rob.

I understood the reason for their anonymity outside the court, but it seemed grossly unfair that Yousef was named publicly, and they were not. His picture had been plastered across the national media, with stories that were often inaccurate, invasive, and deeply hurtful for us. We had been hounded by reporters, to the extent that my own mother, hours after losing her son, was unable to have a cigarette in her own home without being snapped by a photographer. She had even dyed her hair and fled her own home, to escape the spotlight. So why had their families been protected when we had not?

On our second day in the new court, the usher came to inform us that we would have to move upstairs, to sit behind a glass screen, far above the courtroom and quite removed from proceedings.

"What?" I gasped.

I kept my voice low, out of respect, but I simply couldn't believe what we were being asked to do. And in fact, we were not asked; we were told. The defendants' families would remain downstairs, close to their sons. We could not be close to our boy. We were the ones who would have to make way.

"Why should we have to move, and not the defendants' families?" Ghaleb asked. "Why are we being targeted?"

I wasn't sure whether it was simply down to a lack of space in the court or whether the defendants' families had felt uncomfortable sitting so close to us; because we were, after all, the physical and painful reminders of the devastation which had been caused and the reason we were all here. In either case, it seemed so unfair. But this was a court and we had to do as we were told without complaint. Even so, as we climbed the steps to the floor above, it felt as though we were being sidelined; like we were nothing more than an after-thought in the whole process.

Mum struggled to move and make her way to the top floor, her mobility was poor, and I felt a jab of annoyance. Was this the right way to treat a grieving mother? Upstairs, behind the glass screen, we had to strain to hear what was being said, there were headphones but not enough pairs to go around. And we couldn't clearly see everything that was happening. From our position, we were looking down on people's heads. Was this really the best the British justice system could offer us, in a murder trial? My resentment simmered quietly. It wasn't really like me to make a fuss; I was a compliant and accepting person by nature. But more than that, I just didn't have it in me. It was taking every ounce of strength and courage I had just to be here, for Yousef, and to see justice done.

Soon after our move, Mr Johnson QC, for the prosecution, gave his opening statement:

"On Saturday, 2nd March this year – so three and a half months ago – a young man called Yousef Makki was stabbed to death on Gorse Bank Road in Hale Barns. Yousef Makki was born on 28th September, 2001, and therefore he was only 17 when he died. He was stabbed in the heart by his friend, Joshua Molnar, who is the first defendant and sits closest to me. The fatal incident happened at about 25 to seven that Saturday evening. It happened at the conclusion of an afternoon which Yousef, Joshua Molnar and indeed a third lad called Adam Chowdhary, who sits closest to you in the dock, had spent in each other's company…"

I listened, transfixed, as he described how an earlier fight between Joshua Molnar and another group – completely unrelated to Yousef – may have been the trigger for the stabbing. But he also suggested that an alleged plot to rob a drug dealer could have been the catalyst for the stabbing. I was stunned. The evidence was spiralling quickly away into unknown territory. I knew nothing about fights, robberies, or drug deals.

Mr Johnson said: "The emergency services were called very quickly after the stabbing. When the police arrived it will not surprise you to know that they were very interested to know who was responsible for what had happened to Yousef Makki. Both Joshua Molnar and Adam Chowdhary lied to the police when they arrived and they said, both of them, that whilst they had not exactly seen what had happened, the person or people responsible for this injury to Yousef had just left the scene in a small grey Polo car…

"A police officer who attended the scene asked Josh Molnar what had happened. He replied and I quote directly from what he said: 'Yousef has walked ahead. He's fallen and he just started coughing up blood. It was all over him. I took off my shirt and put pressure on it.' The officer pressed Josh Molnar on how the injury had happened and he replied and I quote: 'I don't know. I just came round the corner, and he'd been stabbed. As we came round the corner a car just drove off' and he said the car was possibly a silver VW Polo. When asked what he thought was the motive, he suggested the possibility of robbery, the silver VW Polo plus robbery, the motive according to Josh Molnar to the police for the stabbing of his friend Yousef Makki.

"We suggest, ladies and gentlemen, that Josh Molnar was callously using a real event… hoping to lead the police on a false trail, hoping to avoid responsibility for what he had done."

It was all I could do not to let out an audible gasp in court. Inside my head, I was screaming. Not only had Yousef been stabbed by a friend, but that same friend had then blatantly tried to blame it on someone else.

Earlier on the day of Yousef's death, the court heard that he and the two defendants had been on Booths Car Park and Yousef had been filmed shadow-boxing on CCTV. I didn't understand why that was even relevant. It seemed to me that Yousef was being portrayed in court as a fighter, a working-class boy who could not control his temper, when in reality he saw shadow boxing as a form of fun and entertainment. As a boxer, Yousef was self-disciplined and self-controlled. He was not aggressive, or violent, and he didn't get into fights. Boxing was a way out of trouble, not a way into it. But in court, this was twisted and skewed.

The court was also told that Adam had set up a drug deal, to buy cannabis, and when three men arrived in a grey Polo, he had suggested robbing them – a theory which Adam's defence later disproved. Yousef stood a few metres back and then rode off on his bike with Adam. The man in the grey Polo got the impression that he was about to be robbed because, having refused to hand over the cannabis in absence of payment, Joshua Molnar began to pull at the driver's door, ordering him out of the car. The alleged drug dealer then noticed Joshua Molnar was reaching into the waistband of his trousers and formed the impression he was reaching for a knife. The other two alleged drug dealers got out of the Polo and punched Joshua Molnar. When he escaped, he left his expensive bike behind, and one of the alleged drug dealers threw it over the hedge.

They later caught up with Yousef who spoke with them on civil terms. But the incident left Joshua Molnar furious that his two friends had left him to take a beating and he claimed Yousef had called him a 'pussy' during a bust-up that followed around 90 minutes later that same evening. During the confrontation, on a leafy Cheshire street, Yousef was stabbed to death using a knife which had been bought online. The court was told Joshua Molnar hid the knives down a drain and concocted a story for the police before Adam Chowdhary called 999.

This information left me cold with shock. It was bad enough to know that Yousef had been stabbed by one friend, using a knife which another had bought. But to then hear the charge that Molnar had fabricated a story, trying to blame someone else for the stabbing; it was gut-wrenching. Never in my worst nightmares – and there had been many – had I expected this. The deceptions felt like a set of Russian dolls; each time I pulled the head off one, I discovered a new and more cruel betrayal underneath.

More evidence was heard which suggested that Joshua Molnar was known to one of the alleged drug dealers and had had a previous altercation with them. It was suggested that he was beaten up, not because of a failed robbery, but because of a history of bad blood between them. The motive for the attack on Joshua Molnar – which it seemed had later led to Yousef's death – was not clear. But it appeared to me that Yousef had very little, or nothing, to do with either event.

Mr Webster QC, representing Joshua Molnar, said: "In that brief period of time, literally a minute and a half, something happened between those two 17-year-old friends which changed their lives and the families' lives irrevocably and for the worst. We all know what the event was. A knife held by Mr Molnar entered Yousef Makki's chest; it pierced his heart…

"There had been friction between Adam Chowdhary

and Josh Molnar for reasons you may well understand having heard the evidence. There is no evidence at all, at all, of any confrontation between Josh Molnar and Yousef Makki. No squaring up and no angry gesticulations, and so whatever happened in those one minute and 24 seconds was clearly something which happened quickly in the blink of an eye. It was not anything premeditated. It was not anything long in the making...

"You may have wondered when you see these well-educated children and you see what they were up to with cannabis, juvenile gangster talk and playing around with knives, what is going on with this generation of children? What is going on with them? They have the advantage of good families, a good education, they are clearly materially well off, but they appear to have led a double life, acting out idiotic roles and fantasies, not using their intelligence to evaluate the dangers of what they were doing. You have seen them messing around in the car park, shadow boxing, waiting for the cannabis deal. What a way for talented young kids to be wasting an afternoon. What a way for them to be wasting their lives."

I cringed with embarrassment when I heard there was clear evidence of Yousef smoking cannabis, swearing and using abusive language. He ought to have known better, much better.

But apart from the evidence from the defendants – one of whom had already fabricated a story about the way in which Yousef died – there was no evidence to say that Yousef had a knife. There was no CCTV of Yousef with a knife and there was no DNA on the knives. His blood, of course, was on the blade of the knife which had pierced his heart. The court was told that Adam Chowdhary had ordered and bought the knives online in a false name – he would claim in his defence that he and Yousef bought the knives together – and had them delivered to another address. Joshua Molnar also admitted carrying a knife and there were many videos of him showing off with knives.

Even so, I felt frustrated with Yousef that he had got himself mixed up in a mess like this. This wasn't him. I knew that. But I didn't want the rest of the world to think badly of him, not when he was unable to speak out and defend himself.

MGS had sent representatives to court every day, which was a gesture I really appreciated. But now, my skin crawled with embarrassment. I didn't want them to think of Yousef as a boy who dabbled with knives or drugs. It was one thing smoking a bit of cannabis; I imagined most teenagers tried that at some point or another. But it was another completely to plot to rob an alleged drug dealer or to carry a knife; regardless of how serious the intentions were. That was a whole new level. That said, there was no evidence that Yousef had been involved in a robbery or that he had carried knives, save the testimonies of the two defendants, one of whom – Molnar – had been caught telling lies.

Joshua Molnar's own barrister described Yousef's messages on social media as: "Idiotic, juvenile, pathetic, but not sinister, just stupid."

There was a break in proceedings and, outside in

the corridor, Mum was predictably disappointed and annoyed with Yousef.

"I can't believe the language Yousef used in those messages to his friends," she said. "He never spoke like that at home. I would have wiped the floor with him."

But she knew equally, that in Yousef's case, the language and the bluff was as far as it went. He did not buy or carry knives. He did not take part in robberies or get into serious fights. The defendants and their legal team, however, could say what they liked about Yousef. Because he was dead.

"It's not fair," Maz said angrily. "Yousef was no different to any other teenage boy; they all talk like that. But they're not being serious, they don't follow it through.

"Now that he's dead, he gets the blame for everything and actually, he has done nothing wrong."

I felt for Maz. He was usually so quiet, and the outburst was unexpected, but it was indicative of the stress he was under. He was just a child himself, yet he been through trauma that no adult should ever have to face.

"Yousef will get justice," I reassured him, putting an arm around his shoulders. "Let's focus on the end result."

We went back into court with that thought in mind. And in further evidence we were told that the knife which was used to kill Yousef had been bought online using a false name from an app called Wish. It had cost a total of £4 for two knives. So just £2 for one knife. I felt sickened when the figure was read out in court. Would it have helped if the knife had cost £200? £2000? £200,000? Of course not. But it seemed such a small and paltry amount, negligible almost. It cost £2 to train at Yousef's boxing gym. I remembered, a couple of days before his death, he had wheedled £2 from me to pay for his training session. It was a negligible sum; I could probably find £2 in small change floating around the house or lying in the dust at the bottom of my handbag. Yet that was all it had cost to rip the heart and soul from our family.

I wondered too if the image I had seen on social media, of a knife sent from Adam to Yousef, was in fact the knife which had pierced his heart. The thought sent a chill right through me.

I had provided that image to police, along with countless other images and videos, some portraying Yousef in a positive light, some less so. Yet I had passed them all to the police because it was the right thing to do. At that point, I had hoped that others around me in the investigation might also do the right thing. But I knew now that I had been wrong.

Part way through the fourth day of the evidence, we were shown bodycam footage. Mum had stayed at home today; she was feeling the strain of the trial and her arthritis, doubtless triggered by stress, was crippling her. We had been forewarned that some of the evidence, in particular video footage, would be both graphic and disturbing and I had asked for prior notice so that I could leave the court beforehand. But without any warning, as I sat behind the glass screen, the bodycam footage from the paramedics who had treated Yousef began to play on a large screen in the court in full, 3D, horrifying technicolour. I felt Mazen reach across and grasp my hand, and the kindness almost finished me. I felt raw, open to the elements, pathetically vulnerable.

In the next scene, I spotted Yousef's new white trainers, splattered with blood, sticking out from behind a car, and the grief ballooned inside my chest, suffocating me and cutting off my breath. Those treasured trainers. He had strutted around the house in them, admired himself in the mirror in them, but never could we have imagined that he would die in them. I was struggling to control my sobs, but I felt compelled to stay in court, so that I could report back to Mum later. Yet this wasn't how I wanted to remember my brother.

The next day, Mum came back to court and the recordings of the 999 calls made by Adam Chowdhary were played. During the first call, he asked for the police and could be heard telling the operator "my mate's been stabbed" before giving the address and adding: "He's going to die, please hurry up, please… Please hurry up bro, please."

The court had heard that both the accused had made efforts to stem the bleeding at the scene.

In the recording, Adam Chowdhary was heard to say "breathe, breathe" before telling the 999 operator the injured person was Yousef Makki.

"He's 17. He's a minor," he said, before adding: "He can't breathe properly."

When asked to provide his name, Adam replied: "Is that necessary?" but he then provided his details after being told it was necessary.

Adam then said that Yousef's eyes were closed and

became exasperated when he added: "He's bleeding so much. Get an ambulance."

Moments later he let out a muted scream.

The court heard that during this 999 call Adam Chowdhary made a second 999 call, this time to the ambulance service, using Yousef's mobile phone. During this call he reported someone had been stabbed and urged the call handler to "please hurry up".

He added that blood was "all over" Yousef.

Asked by a member of the emergency services how it happened, Adam replied, on the recording: "I don't know."

He was then asked: "Whereabouts did you say the guy that stabbed your friend go?"

Adam replied: "I don't know, he got off."

"Yeah, but which direction?"

"I don't even know. I didn't even clock it."

"Do you not remember anything?"

"I saw a whip, that's it, a whip, a car."

And later, also recorded, Adam asked: "Can I call my mum? Now that's the only thing I'm worried about, my mum."

He was told: "Now listen mate, your mate's been seriously injured here."

A passer-by and witness, Ben Sallon, told the police: "These guys aren't telling me what's going on."

At that moment, in the court, my vision went fuzzy, and I felt horribly bilious. I was trembling from head to foot, as though an electric pulse was running through me. Again, I felt the reassurance of Mazen's hand over mine, and I steadied myself. But nobody could be expected to sit and listen to a child dying in this way. Mum and I ran from the court, blinded by tears, retching in horror. Outside, we were reassured by our liaison officers, who tried to persuade us to go home for the day. But again, I felt a duty to go back inside the court. I owed it to Yousef.

We also saw bodycam footage from the police officers at the scene, which showed Adam Chowdhary wanting to be allowed to go home and asking: "How long do you think this process will take?"

An officer was heard to tell him: "Do you not think this is a bit of an emergency?"

He replied: "Yes, this is an emergency."

I was dumbfounded. He was supposed to be one of Yousef's best friends. And yet, as Yousef lay dying in the street, Adam asked: "How long do you think this process will take?" Yousef's life and his brutal and lonely death was reduced to a 'process'. I felt my faith slipping.

I remembered hoping, before I knew of the arrests, that Adam was with Yousef when he died, so that his final memory would have been of a friendly face. Now I didn't know what to believe.

Miss Laws QC, in legal argument and in defence of Adam Chowdhary, said: "Perverting the course of justice requires some sort of positive act, a failure to point out an error doesn't suffice. So he was not forthcoming at the scene in relation to much detail and he certainly, even on the prosecution case, couldn't be said to be peddling the same story as Josh Molnar; he was simply saying he didn't see what happened. And, in fact, in contrast to obstructing the police in any way, he was the person who called the police, called the ambulance and spent quite some time with Yousef Makki and also on the phone explaining what was happening with him; he later at the scene pointed out, in fact, where he had kicked the knife that Yousef had held. So that is the evidence at the scene."

The jurors were also shown body-worn video from an officer who escorted Adam Chowdhary back to his home following the stabbing. On the video the officer and Adam Chowdhary sat at a kitchen table as Adam, who had hold of Yousef's glasses, gave an account of events that night. The officer said: "We need to find out what happened don't we?" Adam, who had blood on his hands, broke down in tears.

It shook me, most of all, that Adam had Yousef's glasses in his hand. It was a small detail, but it crucified me, and I found it hard to take.

The pathologist who had examined Yousef's body gave a statement, saying that Yousef was 180 centimetres tall and weighed 71 kilos, which is about 5' 11" and 11st. 2lbs. As he spoke, I could see Yousef so clearly in my mind's eye; tall, slim and handsome. But hearing about him in the past tense, described almost as a specimen, an exhibit, was very hard. It felt so impersonal and so remote. He was being presented as a cardboard cut-out, two-dimensional and without character or soul. I wanted to shout out: "He was teaching his nephew to play the ukulele! He loved chilli-flavoured crisps! He hated wearing glasses because he thought it put the girls off! He was a real person! None of you know him!"

But of course I said nothing.

They did not know Yousef and they certainly did not have the slightest inkling of the absolute heartbreak and nuclear devastation his death had wrought in our lives.

There was a statement too from the surgeon who lived near the scene of the stabbing and had rushed outside to try to save Yousef. He had in fact performed a 'clamshell thoracotomy' which involved cutting Yousef's chest open in the back of the ambulance to gain access to his internal organs to save him.

But the stab wound had been 12cms deep, passing through Yousef's heart and out of the other side, with the hilt of the knife bruising against his chest. His death had been bloody and doubtless he was petrified and in unimaginable pain. Despite the frantic and well-meaning efforts of the people who tried to help, he had died.

To my surprise, the court heard that Yousef was wearing a black The North Face bubble coat and grey Stone Island cargo pants, when he died. The coat was slashed open, with the knife. These weren't his clothes; Mum could not afford labels like that. I could only assume that having slept over at Adam's the previous night, he had then borrowed some of his clothes. The realisation was stomach-turning.

Each day of the court case brought fresh horror, fresh trauma. The detail was at times vile and lurid, other times utterly heartbreaking. But each day, Mazen and I got up out of bed like battery-operated robots, fed the children, took them to school and nursery, and made our way to court on the tram.

We did not miss a single day. In the evenings, we were exhausted and drained, our minds swamped, our brains addled, by the arguments and counter-arguments we had listened to all day. It was too much effort even to speak. It was perhaps 6pm by the time we were home after collecting the children and cooking a meal, then 7pm when they were settled down with baths and bedtime stories.

Again, at those times, the children were a wonderful diversion, because for a short period at least we could talk about Postman Pat and fishfingers and chips and bubble baths. The relief was splendid, yet temporary and brittle. Those moments with my children, those snatched sections of normality, kept me sane.

For the rest of the evening, when the children were asleep, Mazen and I were almost catatonic and mute with shock. And even at weekends, it felt like an inevitable countdown to Monday morning, to the next onslaught. There was no escape.

23

At the last minute, we were told that Adam Chowdhary would not be taking the stand to give evidence, though his interview with the police would be read to the court. I understood that not taking the stand was his legal right, but I found it frustrating and deeply disappointing. I wanted to hear from him in person; I wanted to hear all about Yousef's last moments in this world; how he had looked, what he had said. However soul-destroying, I needed to hear it from him. It was not much to ask, given our tragedy.

Joshua Molnar gave evidence in person however, and he claimed that Yousef not only had a knife but had also given him a knife. In his statement, he said: "He came towards me. I pulled the knife Yousef had given me. I moved my arm forward with the knife in my hand. I think he came on to the knife, which must have made things worse. I was acting in self-defence.

"We both realised what had happened. I became upset. I started crying and I was walking up and down the road. I then realised it was serious. Yousef was coughing up blood. I took off clothing and ripped open my T-shirt to push it against the wound. Adam dialled 999. A security guard came to our aid. We waited for the emergency services.

"In panic and whilst we were waiting, me and Adam agreed to make up a story about Yousef being attacked while we were round the corner. (Molnar later admitted this was a lie and that Adam was not involved in making up the story).

"At some point I hid the two knives near a bush. I don't know what happened to Yousef's knife. I now want to tell the truth about what happened. I'm absolutely devastated and I am in shock. Can I also apologise about talking about Yousef as if he's still alive. I'm only too aware that he is not."

The prosecution went on to say: "Well, ladies and gentlemen, we suggest that in that prepared statement he was not telling the truth or anything like it. Far from it. He was blaming Yousef Makki for having both flick knives and suggesting that Yousef Makki had attacked him with a knife. He was saying Adam had not had a knife, but subsequent police enquiries revealed it was Adam who had bought the knives. Not only had he bought the knives but he had had them delivered in a false name to somebody else's address. Earlier that afternoon police had searched the area of the incident in Gorse Bank Road."

Speaking of the moments before the stabbing, under cross-examination, Joshua Molnar said: "I was getting a bit more angry, so I'd said: 'Fuck off, I'm going home.' Then I believe Yousef's got a bit annoyed with me. He's called… he's called me a pussy. I… I've got annoyed at this, because obviously I was the only one that was stood there and got a beating, whilst one of my friends ran off and the other one kind of just watched… I didn't think it was fair. I said: 'How am I a pussy if I'm the one that's stood there and taking a beating whilst you two kind of done nothing?' This is when I've pushed Yousef… just out of frustration. It was just with the palm. I just kind of pushed him kind of like, just like… It wasn't like I'd gone with full force. It was just kind of like, 'I'm not in the mood, go away. Just leave me alone…' He got annoyed about that. He's then… he's then hit me. Just his… his hand. He just punched me."

Molnar told the court he had opened the blade on his knife to warn Yousef off. But when asked if he knew how the knife had ended up inside Yousef, he replied: "Not really, no. I do… I do know what I did. I don't know how it all came together…

"Well, I'm trying to get my knife out of my pocket. I'm a bit disorientated at the time, so I'm kind of… I'm kind of struggling. I can't remember if Yousef either kind of like laughed a bit or if he said something, but I just got more annoyed, so I've kind of like, I've brought it out with quite a bit of speed, as in like I've not just taken it out and then stood there. I've kind of just taken it out straightaway, and I don't really know what I did. I just kind of lifted my arm up. I didn't realise anything had really happened at first.

"I just… Yousef kind of just took a step back, so I kind of just thought he'd seen me do this and he just wanted to take a step back… He, he stepped back after I brought it out. This is after what's happened has happened… I didn't really think it was anything at first. I didn't think I'd stabbed him… I'd kind of started to walk away. Then

Yousef calls out, saying something like, like… 'You stabbed me.' At that point I kind of just went into a bit of a panic. I was kind of just in the middle of the road. I don't really know what I was thinking. I was just a bit panicked."

Joshua Molnar claimed he did not know the knife ended up in Yousef and that he had not intended to cause him any harm.

He told the court: "I personally don't think it's massively important who gave me the knife or when, but it's just my opinion."

Just hearing him speak, imagining Yousef in those final moments, the pain, the fear, the panic he must have felt, was soul-destroying. My heart was pounding as I listened to the voice of Joshua Molnar, the voice of the person who had killed my brother. I had a marble of stress jammed so hard in my throat that I could not swallow or breathe. Time seemed to stop; suspended, as he spoke. At one point, he even wiped away a few tears.

But they didn't convince me.

Joshua Molnar, who was from an extraordinarily wealthy and privileged background, was also asked under cross-examination about photos and videos which appeared to show his obsession with knives. In one, he had climbed scaffolding and was holding a knife. He said he thought it looked cool.

He said: "It was a strange shaped knife that looked aesthetically pleasing," and he confirmed he had taken the video of himself. A second video showed him lighting a spliff with a flare.

He said: "It was just after Hallowe'en and a friend had some flares and fireworks left over… It was just a bit of fun going out to smoke a zoot."

He admitted throwing a flare near a car. He said it would not result in an explosion or any damage, and agreed it was a stupid thing to do but at the time it was just a bit of fun.

He was then shown a video in a bedroom in which he waved a long knife or machete at another boy and poked at the mattress with it. Another video showed him laughing and slashing at his friend. The court also heard allegations that, a year before Yousef was killed, Joshua Molnar had gatecrashed a party at a £1m mansion in Hale Barns and, when a fight broke out, he punched a boy before pulling a blade from his waistband, terrifying the other guests.

I was appalled. If this evidence was accurate, Joshua Molnar had been using knives and frightening people long before he stabbed Yousef. This was a tragedy waiting to happen. A bomb waiting to explode. Yousef was quite possibly, quite simply, in the wrong place at the wrong time.

The prosecution also summarised Adam Chowdhary's statement, saying: "He said that Joshua had had two knives on him at the time, one of which Joshua had taken from him, Adam, earlier that day.

"The only evidence in the case as to whether or not Yousef Makki had a knife comes from the defendants."

The court heard that Adam filmed himself brandishing a flick knife and sent the video to Yousef.

I felt a fury bubbling inside me as I listened to the statements from Adam and Joshua. Yousef was not here to defend himself. He had no voice to prove or disprove their version of events on that dark day. He had no say at all in this. I was not normally an angry or even a demonstrative person; I was naturally very peaceful and timid. But in that moment, I wanted to stand on my chair and scream. The injustice was hard to swallow.

And there was worse to come. For though Adam Chowdhary decided not to take the stand, he was allowed to call two character witnesses who gave lengthy statements in his favour.

One said: "In my experience, Adam is a kind, friendly, intelligent young man, who was a pleasure to teach and converse with. Adam was in ways very polite, respectful and well-balanced for his age. I'll never forget the time he helped to raise funds for me, with the help of his father, to alleviate the suffering of people in Libya, my home country, during the 2011 revolution. Despite his young age at the time, Adam was very motivated to help others in their times of trouble, who were less fortunate than him. Adam was a very decent, hard-working, respectable young man."

Another said: "I'd describe Adam as an extremely pleasant young man. I always found him a polite and well-mannered individual. Adam is both generous and kind and would go out of his way to extend his hospitality to family and friends. On occasions when I have had conversations with Adam, for example, giving him lifts to school. He's shown a great deal of respect to those around him, he's always displayed a very caring nature and, at times, shown naivety as he only sees goodness in people as a direct result of his upbringing."

The next day, I asked if we could bring some character witnesses for Yousef, to talk about what a lovely young man he was. But the prosecution lawyers told me that wasn't possible.

"You're not allowed to do that for the victim," they said.

I asked again, believing there must have been some misunderstanding, and was again refused. It seemed staggeringly unfair that the defendant was allowed to have people speak for him and yet the victim was not. Yousef's teachers from MGS also asked if they could speak for him; they too felt it was strangely unequal. But they were not allowed to either. We were told that our only opportunity to speak for Yousef as a family would be in the form of a victim impact statement from Mum, at the end of the trial, if and when the defendants were convicted. It seemed both farcical and maddening to me that Yousef, who was supposed to be the focal point of the trial, should be silenced completely. But though I didn't agree with the ruling, I accepted it and respected it, and didn't make a fuss. I did not see it as a sinister portent; another rumble of thunder, signalling the almighty storm which lay on the horizon ahead.

The trial continued and we attended every day, 10am until 4pm. It was both physically and mentally draining. There were reporters and photographers outside the courts each morning, but now, they were very respectful towards us, and left us completely alone. Gone were the photographers hiding behind bushes and sneaking down the side of our house for a quick picture. And though we came face to face with the defendants' families more than once, in the areas outside court, we kept our distance and our dignity.

I noticed, in the court buildings, that they were given their own private rooms to use during breaks and lunchtimes, whilst we had to wait in the corridors outside. It was often difficult for Mum to stand up for any period of time, given her arthritis. Sometimes, too, we were upset and in tears, and we needed somewhere private to calm down. We requested a room ourselves but were told there was nothing available. The defendants had a room. We did not. Again, it seemed like a glaring imbalance but again, I tried to ignore it and instead fled to the ladies' toilets every time I felt a wave of grief overwhelming me.

One day, I found myself behind Adam's family in the coffee shop during a break. I wanted so much to ask them about Yousef and for them to share those final moments with me. This was my chance. Perhaps it was my only chance. The desire to speak burned in my throat. But I didn't say a word. In court, Yousef had been portrayed thus far as the council house boy, the outsider without money or influence or good breeding. I didn't want to let him down by getting into an argument and slotting into the stereotype that had been so meticulously prepared for us.

Joshua Molnar's family had what looked to be a private security firm ushering them in and out of court, which was almost laughable when I thought of Mazen and me jumping onto the crowded tram each morning. But we needed no reminding of the gulf between us. And the more I heard about Joshua Molnar, the wider I wished that gulf could be. He had been moved from school to school, he had a background of cannabis use and a bizarre obsession with knives. He was a liar. He had stabbed Yousef through the heart. So no, the gulf could never be too wide.

After each day of evidence, Yousef's name and photograph were plastered across the regional and national media. It was reported that he had been involved, on the periphery, in a drug deal, when in actual fact there had been no hard evidence to confirm that. Yousef had not been involved in ordering or paying for or collecting any drugs, nor was he involved in the alleged robbery. Again, the two defendants had the cloak of anonymity wrapped around them whilst Yousef, the victim, took all the flak. It left a bitter taste with me. Foolishly perhaps, I had not realised I would feel so much injustice about the justice system.

With each item of evidence, and as the weeks wore on, some pieces of the jigsaw slowly slotted together. We now knew that Yousef had been essentially connected with the 'double lives' led by Adam Chowdhary and Joshua Molnar, who had indulged in drugs and carried knives against a backdrop of entitlement, living in one of the country's most affluent postcodes. Their 'idiotic fantasies' had come to a head when the trio were hanging around in Hale Barns. CCTV showed Yousef shadow-boxing. (This, to me, seemed to be the main criticism of Yousef in the court.) From there the three of them rode off to another rendezvous where

Adam Chowdhary had arranged to buy cannabis. There was then a suggestion – which was later disproved by the defence lawyers – of a plot to rob the alleged drug dealers, which ended with Yousef and Adam Chowdhary fleeing, and Joshua Molnar taking a beating. We knew also that there was apparently previous bad feeling between Joshua Molnar and the alleged dealers. Later, angry that he had lost his bike and angry that his friends had deserted him, Joshua Molnar and Yousef had argued. Yousef was stabbed through the heart – inexplicably, violently, fatally. And in the moments afterwards one of his loyal friends concocted a plan to try to put the blame elsewhere. Yes, Adam had called for help, and they had tried to stem the bleeding. But when the police came, they did not get a clear picture.

Yet by the end of it all, we were still left, frustratingly, with so many missing parts. There was no clear overall picture. We didn't even know the precise motive for Yousef's death, or even if there was one. How did a minor disagreement between two friends escalate into a fatal stabbing? I realised, in despair, that we would never probably know the real truth. And somewhere, in between the lies and the half-truths, the self-pity and the self-preservation, there was the death of a boy. Our boy.

Finally, after more than three weeks, the court case drew to a close. In her closing speech, Miss Laws QC, defending Adam, said: "He had not been in trouble with the police before, not ever. You know that, notwithstanding the privilege of having a good education, he had started to take risks and made some serious mistakes.

"On the day in question, you know that he was purchasing, or about to purchase, and smoke cannabis. You know that he had purchased and was taking out a knife, and that this is behaviour he had been keeping secret, completely secret, from his family. All that now is out in the open for all of us to see, and you know that his behaviour, or the start of it, led to the chain of events, the completely unforeseeable tragic death of his best friend. And, as one of his character witnesses rightly says, he has to live with his contribution to Yousef Makki's death for the rest of his life. It was he, after all, who had purchased the knife... but he is not on trial for buying the knife or taking it out with him. He has pleaded guilty to that; he will be punished...

"He is not on trial for arranging to purchase some cannabis. None of them are on trial for that no matter how reprehensible, how incomprehensible it is and, indeed, illegal, but it is the sorry background to this case that you have heard about. Nor is he on trial for being a coward; for, once the violence started, fleeing... He is not on trial for that. Remember, he did not stab Yousef Makki. He is not on trial for the bad decisions he made..."

Molnar's lawyer spoke as well but I felt a rush of anticipation, knowing that justice was almost in touching distance. I had stayed strong, day after day, blow after blow and the finishing line was almost in sight. The expectation swelled inside me, for soon, we would have justice for the brother we loved and had lost. After the judge had finished his summing up, the jury was sent out to deliberate.

"What shall we do?" I asked Mazen. "Where shall we go?"

I was on tenterhooks, unable to make the simplest of decisions. I didn't want to stray too far from the court, because we knew we had to be back at a moment's notice, yet neither did I want to hang around in the corridors like a stray animal, unworthy of a private room.

In the end, we took Maz to a coffee shop, and then we milled around Crown Square, feeling at once exhausted and wired; hopeless and yet filled with hope that we would soon feel comfort and closure at the verdict. There would be no elation, no triumph. But there would be justice. Late in the afternoon, after almost an entire day, we got the call to say the jury was coming back. The verdict was in.

"Quickly, quickly," I said to Maz. "Let's run!"

We abandoned our coffees and dashed back into court, breathless and hot, for it was another sunny day. The lifts were almost full, so Mum squeezed in, and instead we sprinted up the stairs, two at a time, the blood rushing through my veins and thundering in my ears.

By the time we got into our seats, in the high glass box, the jury was already back in court. I had only a few seconds to compose myself before I heard the clerk ask: "Do you find the defendant Joshua Molnar guilty or not guilty on Count 1 of murder?"

And then, it was as if I was falling, faster and faster, off my seat and down a long tunnel. Everything became echoey and distant as the wind screamed around my ears.

"Not guilty."

"On the alternative offence of manslaughter, do you find him guilty or not guilty?

"Not guilty."

I heard a female voice shout: "What?" and I didn't even know whether it was my voice or someone else's. Around me, in slow motion, the faces of the people I loved were crumpled in pain, distorted in defeat and disbelief. In the background, like a death knell, like a dagger through my soul, it went on:

"Do you find Joshua Molnar guilty or not guilty of conspiracy to rob?"

"Not guilty."

"Do you find Adam Chowdhary guilty or not guilty of conspiracy to rob?"

"Not guilty."

"Do you find Adam Chowdhary guilty or not guilty of doing an act tending and intended to pervert the course of justice?"

"Not guilty."

Chaos erupted. Volcanic rage and grief. We were trapped high up, behind the glass screen, like curious exhibits in a zoo. Now, like wild animals, we began banging on the glass, sobbing and screaming. I felt as though I was losing control; the fury choking me back and spurring me on in equal measure. For a moment, I caught sight of myself, of my family around me, looking in from the outside. And I was horrified. We were like a wild rabble. This was not our way. This was not how we behaved. Yet this was what we had been reduced to; thrust into. We had been painted as uneducated and unworldly and now we were being forced to live up to the myth. Like cornered animals, poked with sticks, we snarled and spat and we fought back. Beside me, Ghaleb collapsed, unconscious, in a heap. Mazen ran from his seat, screaming. Yousef's friends were weeping and shouting; disorientated and enraged. We were escorted from the courtroom and the building as though we were a foul and inconvenient smell, as though we belonged outside, in the gutter. Mum was hysterical, sobbing with her head in her hands. Mazen ran towards the defence barristers, shouting: "Filthy money! Filthy money!"

Within seconds, he was surrounded by police. I watched, in despair, as he sank to his knees, tears streaming down his face. Mazen had cried on the night when Yousef was killed but he had not cried since, not until now. He had remained so strong for us all. But in this moment, he was a man in pieces. Everyone has a breaking point. The paramedics arrived and began treating Ghaleb in the back of an ambulance. The police were ushering us all back, herding us, like sheep. Even outside, in the bright, blinding, sunshine, the atmosphere was charged and vengeful. In all the chaos, Adam Chowdhary and his family climbed into a flash 4x4 and drove swiftly away, leaving the whole horrendous mess behind them.

I thought back to Yousef's first day at grammar school, when we had waited as a family at the bus stop, and the chauffeur-driven cars had rolled past us without a second glance. We didn't matter then, and we didn't matter now. I had never felt so small and so insignificant. I felt as though I had been crushed between a finger and a thumb, like a flea. I could not understand – and never would understand

– how my brother had been stabbed to death and yet criminally nobody was to blame. He had been killed, he had been snatched away, aged 17, yet it was nobody's fault. How could that be right? How could that be justice? I remembered that first day, discovering that the defendants had been given a tour around the court. *And we had not.* I remembered too that we had been moved upstairs, behind a glass screen. *And they had not.* All too vividly I recalled my conversation with the prosecution barrister when I wanted Yousef to have character witnesses, as Adam Chowdhary did. *No, not allowed.* And also the exchange with the usher when we had requested a private room. *No, not allowed.* It was all leading to this. "I'm sorry, Yousef," I whispered.

I felt as though we had let him down. All of us. He wasn't here and it was up to us – every single one of us – to do the right thing by him. Somewhere in all the mayhem our liaison officer, Kath, found me and encircled me in a hug.

"We don't think it's a good idea for your Mum and Maz to go home," she said. "There will be so much media interest. We're worried about protests too. People are very angry."

She arranged a hotel for the night for them both. Mum's hysteria had eased but now she was completely white, drained of colour, of fight, of life. She looked so far away; suspended in a shocked stupor.

"Try and get some rest in the hotel," I said to her gently. "I'm sorry, Mum, I really am."

As a grieving mother, she had been failed and failed and failed again. I texted a friend and asked her to collect the boys from school and nursery for me, because I didn't want them to see Mazen and me upset and in such a state. We waited for the tram home, dejected and deflated, and hardly spoke a word to each other on the journey. The silence was stretched taut between us like a tightrope; heavy with everything we wanted to say but could not. Around us, people were commuting home from work, planning a barbeque maybe, a few drinks on a sunny evening, a visit to the park with their children. But my life felt as though it had just been blown apart by a nail bomb. As though someone had thrown a hand grenade right through my existence. I didn't know how or if we would ever return to any kind of normality.

"Maybe this is how it is," Mazen said to me eventually. "Maybe this is how justice works in the UK."

I shook my head numbly and shrugged. I had no idea. After all, this was our first experience of the courts. Perhaps we had been extraordinarily and risibly naive in expecting justice for a boy like Yousef – a working-class Muslim boy of colour from a council estate. Perhaps he simply didn't figure when it came to the crunch. As a teenager, Yousef had been all about the quest for labels, mostly, tantalisingly, out of his reach; Armani, The North Face, Stone Island. Now in death, he had new labels, and each one stung like a slap in the face. Mixed Race. Council House. Working-Class.

I gathered myself together before collecting the children from my friend's house.

"You shouldn't accept that verdict," she said to me angrily. "It's not fair." And when I got home, there were more messages of support, more emotional reactions. On social media, there was a tsunami of outrage and protest. "Maybe we should do something," I said to Mazen. "But what?"

Greater Manchester Police made a statement and called for calm after the hearing.

"Although we are disappointed in today's verdict, we must respect the decision of the jury," said Detective Chief Inspector Colin Larkin.

"I know people in the community may be shocked and upset, but I would urge people to be respectful of Yousef's family and their feelings as they come to terms with today's conclusion.

"Our main focus will be providing support to the family, and we will be engaging with the Crown Prosecution Service over the coming days to consider the next steps to take with our investigation."

All night long, I lay wide awake in bed, becoming more and more determined and focussed that we could not simply let this go, as though Yousef was worth nothing. The verdict was seismic; it had shaken the foundations not only of our family but sent shockwaves right across the city and far beyond. The following day, I saw comments from Manchester MP Lucy Powell in the media questioning whether the verdicts would have been different if the defendants had been of a different social class or of different ethnicity.

"You do have to ask if these defendants were black, at state school and from, say, Moss Side, whether they would have been acquitted," she said on Twitter.

Her words lit a fire inside me. I started to think that we could and should fight against this. Friends and family rallied around us and there was a flood of support both from public figures and the community across Manchester and beyond. We called a meeting, at our house, and our close friends, Ameena and Riz took charge. Their son, Daanish, was one of Yousef's dearest friends.

"I think we should boycott the sentencing, to show that we don't recognise the verdict of the courts," Mazen said.

Everyone agreed with this, and we decided instead to organise a peaceful protest, the day before the sentencing, which was listed for ten days later. The protest would take place outside the Crown Court, outside the very building where my brother had been so badly failed. We each had specific roles, Mum and Ghaleb agreed to speak at the protest, I would address the media and Mazen would request and attend meetings with the police and CPS. Around me, friends began designing posters, ordering wristbands, drawing up a schedule. I was frozen; paralysed, as though the world was whirring round at a much faster speed than normal, and I could no longer keep up. I still could not believe what had happened. But then someone said:

"We need a face for the protest, we need a focus for the campaign, a centre point."

And another voice said: "I'm sorry to say, I think we need a white face, to be taken more seriously."

It was a sad observation, but understandable, given what we had just witnessed. It was felt by everyone at the meeting that a black face would not be afforded the same credibility or respect. Unpalatable, unacceptable, but probably and tragically true. We had lost faith in the justice system and, to some extent, in a society which had allowed that system to exist without question or challenge. Everyone turned towards me.

"Jade, will you do it?" they asked.

I frowned reluctantly and bowed my head. I was shy and quiet, and reeling from the aftershocks of the verdict. I wasn't at all sure about fronting a campaign or leading a protest. I just wasn't that sort of person. Besides, I didn't understand what was required or if I'd even be capable. I was a busy young mum. I'd worked in a nursery, and I was good with children, but I hadn't the first idea about mounting a campaign.

"I'm not sure," I hesitated. "I don't want to mess it up."

"Jade, you can do it," Mazen said loyally. "I know you can. And Yousef would want you to."

'He's right, you'll be fantastic! Think how strict you were when you had to get me up for school each morning! You're scary when you want to be! You can do it, no sweat.'

And so, the decision was made. From somewhere, I found the resolve to parcel away my shock and anger and look forwards. For the posters, I chose a photo of Yousef which he liked. I remembered him saying:

'I look like Sinatra on this, don't you think?'

I had laughed as he joked and preened and admired his own photo.

"You're so vain!" I'd told him. "It's all that time spent in front of the mirror, doing your hair. You're in love with yourself!"

He had really loved that photo. So I knew he'd approve of

my choice. We decided the poster should be of Yousef's face only, with the slogan: 'Justice for Yousef Makki' underneath.

'I'm famous! Trending on twitter! Loads of shares!'

We wanted to do everything by the book, with no room for criticism, and so we applied for formal permission from the police to stage a protest.

"You'll need stewards," we were told.

"That's easily done," I replied.

I bought a job lot of yellow tabards from eBay and handed them out amongst Yousef's friends. I was confident there would be no trouble. Yousef just wasn't that type of boy, and this just wasn't that type of protest.

"Wear these please," I smiled.

And that was how it went from there. Every time someone tried to put an obstacle in my path, I felt the fight swelling up inside me. I was energised; glowing inside with a passion. I owed this to Yousef. I owed it to every boy who had been forgotten and failed by the justice system. The morning of the protest dawned, and it was forecast to be boiling hot weather again. Over breakfast, I nibbled half-heartedly at a slice of toast as the children chattered around me.

"What if nobody turns up?" I said worriedly to Mazen.

"It doesn't matter at all," Mazen replied. "We are here for him and that is what counts. Stop worrying."

Not for the first time, I gave silent thanks that I had a husband like Mazen; supportive, strong, sensible, and the emotional scaffolding I relied upon every day.

"You're right," I nodded.

Today, I was wearing bright colours. Today, I was determined to smile. Because today was all about Yousef.

We took the three children with us, lugging the double pram onto the tram, with Raafat skipping alongside us. As I took my seat, I spotted a lady who used to babysit for Mum, many years earlier. I thought it was just a coincidence, but she said to me:

"I'm on my way to the protest. I saw what happened to your brother and I think it's a disgrace. I want to offer my support."

Her kindness touched and melted me in a way that no anger ever could, and I found myself biting back the tears.

"Thank you," I whispered.

As we arrived at Crown Square, we saw there were already groups of people gathering. More arrived, more than we had expected and more than we could possibly have dreamed. There were maybe about 300 people there. Yousef's school friends wore T-shirts with his photo on the front.

We had invited the press too and they were there in numbers. And it wasn't just working-class people from council estates, like us. There were residents from Hale Barns, the wealthy suburb where Yousef had died. There was a complete cross section of colours, cultures and social groups.

Our aim was not to polarise, to vilify, or to divide. We wanted change, not conflict. Everyone was welcome. The only distinction that mattered was quite simply the difference between right and wrong. As I pushed the double pram amongst the crowd, I could hear Yousef's voice on my shoulder. *'Well done, sis. Knew you could do it. I'm proud of you.'*

"You too," I whispered.

The crowd were singing protest songs: 'We will Overcome' and chanting: 'No Justice, no peace, no justice, no peace.' It was like a drum beat inside my head. There was a makeshift stage and in turn various people made speeches, through a megaphone. Ghaleb gave a speech and then Mum stepped up too.

"I will never give up the fight for justice for my son," she said tearfully. "Never."

I was in awe of her; I knew it took a lot out of her. Raafat, 10, stood at my side, mesmerised by the booming sound of the loudspeaker.

"Can I have a turn?" he asked, pulling at my sleeve.

"Oh no darling, not today," I replied.

"I want to speak, I want to tell everyone about Uncle Yo-Yo," he insisted, slipping his little hand in mine. He wasn't at all nervous. He was confident, self-assured and focussed. In many ways, he reminded me so much of Yousef.

"Today isn't the right time," I said.

But then I looked at the faces around me, over 300 of them; politicians, community leaders, celebrities. And, most importantly, families. Ordinary, decent, families who were outraged and appalled by the idea that it might be possible to buy your way through the British justice system. They were here to support us. They were here to give Yousef a voice. My Yousef, my brother; the boy from the council estate with the pound coin in his pocket. He did not stand a chance against the wealth and privilege which brought him down.

And I realised it was exactly the right time.

I watched, my heart simultaneously breaking and bursting with pride, as my 10-year-old son climbed onto the make-shift stage and took the megaphone in his hands. He was not even strong enough to hold it, and, as it wobbled and the crowd held a collective breath, Mazen ran on stage to help him out.

Raafat looked out across the sea of faces, his small face tight with grief, anger and determination. And in him, suddenly, I saw hope, shining like golden strands of gossamer, way ahead; too far for me to reach out and touch it. But I knew it was there. And in that moment, I knew I could fight this.

"Justice for Yousef Makki!" Raafat shouted, his tiny voice carrying across the courthouse square and beyond, into the city centre. "Justice for my uncle!"

In that epiphanic moment, our campaign: 'Justice For Yousef Makki' was born.

The protest lasted three hours, and as we gave out leaflets and wristbands and listened to speeches and songs, many more passers-by came to join us. That night, at home, we watched and listened as the protest made the regional and national TV and radio news. It was reported across print media too and online.

"We did a good thing today," Mazen told me, wrapping his arms around me. "But this is only the start."

24

The next day, we refused to attend the sentencing as planned, instead waiting at home for the news to come in. Joshua Molnar had admitted perverting the course of justice by lying to police and possession of a flick knife. He had been cleared of murder and an alternative count of manslaughter. Adam Chowdhary was cleared of perverting the course of justice by allegedly lying to police about what he had seen, but also admitted possession of a flick knife. Both had been cleared of conspiracy to commit robbery in the lead-up to Yousef's death. Both defendants, who had been granted bail, faced sentencing for possession of the flick knives, and Joshua faced sentence for perverting the course of justice.

Mr Justice Bryan told the boys: "There is a price to pay for your actions."

He spoke of a 'warped' knife culture, in which carrying a blade is considered 'cool'.

The sentencing was reported on social media even before the police had chance to call me.

"They've been sent to a young offenders' institute," Mazen announced, refreshing his phone.

Mr Justice Bryan sentenced Joshua Molnar to a 12-month detention and training order for perverting the course of justice; and a four-month detention and training order for possessing a bladed article, to run consecutively – 16 months in total. Adam Chowdhary was sentenced to a four-month detention and training order. The first two months would be served in custody.

Justice Bryan told them: "The backdrop to your offending is depressingly all too familiar. A warped culture whereby the possession of knives is considered to be 'cool' and 'aesthetically pleasing', and knives are routinely carried on our streets.

"Mix that with youth as well as drugs and drug dealing, as in the present case, and it is a recipe for disaster and the tragic, but all too predictable, events that unfolded on the early evening of March 2nd, 2019, with the loss of the young life of your friend Yousef Makki who had everything to live for, and the irreparable harm that resulted, which has changed the lives of his family and friends forever...

"From the evidence I have heard in the course of your trial it is clear that both of you had an unhealthy fixation with knives which is all too common amongst the youth of today. It must stop. There is nothing cool about knives.

"Their carrying all too often leads to their use and to tragedy, and it is a fallacy that they can keep you safe – very much the reverse, as events all too often demonstrate. Knife crime is a canker on society, and it affects all spectrums of society – the message that must be brought home is that knives kill, and knives ruin lives.

"You will both have to live with your actions that day and the consequences of the same for the rest of your lives. That is a different form of sentence to the sentences that I can and must pass in respect of the offending to which you have pleaded guilty…

"The best legacy of Yousef's tragic death would be if this message could be got across – and knives regarded as 'uncool' by the young in society going forward…

"There is a price to pay for your actions. I can only hope that other young people in your position will learn from your mistakes and will be put off taking knives onto the streets."

Reading the judge's comments, I felt a peculiar mix of sorrow and relief. We were the ones with the price to pay. We were the ones with the life sentence. I took no joy in the sentencing, none at all. And yet, it was a tiny scrap of comfort that the defendants had at least been sent to a youth offenders institute. We were later told that public pressure, and the peaceful protest, had probably helped to ensure that. A few months locked up was nothing to most people, yet at the same time, it was something to me. Moments after the sentencing was made public, I was contacted by various media outlets asking if I would be interviewed with my reactions.

"Absolutely," I replied. "I'm on my way."

All through the trial I had kept my dignity, keeping my thoughts and my feelings to myself. I had stayed silent, I had been compliant and passive, and for what? How had that helped? So now, I felt I had nothing to lose by speaking out. I arranged to meet with reporters outside the crown court. Mazen had to stay at home to look after the children, so I took the tram, on my own, into the city centre. It was another hot day, and I could feel a trickle of nervous sweat running between my shoulder blades. In a frenzy, I fished an old shopping list out of my handbag and began scribbling down some phrases on the back of the paper. I suddenly felt terribly ill-equipped and inadequate; I wasn't sure I could speak to the press. I was a mother, a housewife. I was not a campaign manager or a public speaker. I had made a foolish mistake by agreeing to this. My confidence was slipping away with every tram stop.

"Yousef would do this no problem! Raafat would do this no problem," I told myself firmly. "Stop being such a wuss."

But somehow that just made me feel more incompetent, more out of my depth. And, as I approached Crown Square, I spotted a huge gaggle of reporters, cameras and microphones and my stomach flipped. I was shaking so much that my teeth were chattering.

'Come on, Jade. Pull yourself together. You need to pretend you're trying to get me out of bed for school. Wear your stern face!'

Weak with nerves, I walked towards the waiting pack with my mind racing. In panic I realised I had forgotten everything I wanted to say. My mind was an awful blank. The shopping list was screwed up in the ball of my hand, the ink running as my palms sweated. I couldn't possibly rely on that now. For a split second, I was almost tempted to turn and run. *'Jade! No!'* But then, the Granada TV reporter emerged from the group, and I saw that beneath his smart shirt and tie he was wearing shorts and sandals. I took one look at his odd outfit and started to laugh.

"It's too hot for a full suit," he blushed. "I just hope the cameraman doesn't film my knobbly knees!"

That put me at ease, and I began to relax.

'See! You just have to believe in yourself! Always your problem!'

When I heard a voice speaking passionately and clearly, right across the square, I could hardly believe it was mine. I had no notes, no prompts, and yet, I knew exactly what I wanted to say.

"Whatever punishment was handed out today would never have been enough. He could have got 25 years, but he got 16 months. At least he is going to jail. We all took a stance that we weren't coming today. It is not enough. In a matter of months they will be out and back on the street and back with their families. We are never going to get Yousef back.

"At the moment knife crime is terrifying, especially in Manchester. Four months for carrying a knife? I think it is not enough.

"We will work to change the law around carrying knives and we will work towards justice. We want to prevent other families from going through this. This has to stop."

Afterwards, though I was still trembling, I felt a small glow inside. I felt as though I was doing something for Yousef. Something the courts and the justice system had not done.

Later that day, we were offered a meeting with the police, barristers, and CPS.

"They don't like the fuss we're making," Mazen said to me. "I imagine they want us to be quiet."

And he was right. We arrived at a smart building in the city centre, only to be greeted with a line of sympathetic nods and empty platitudes. Harshly perhaps, I decided these people were not here to do the right thing. They were here to be seen to be doing the right thing.

"There's nothing more we can do," they said. "We have to accept the results of the trial, however hard that is."

Anger welled inside me. This was becoming a familiar feeling now for me. The police seemed to me to be more upset about their crime figures and their strike rates than about Yousef himself.

"There is everything we can do," I snapped, my voice dripping with such contempt I hardly recognised myself. "Everything. Yousef is not a statistic. He is not another case. He is everything to us."

"You have to accept the decision of the jury," insisted one of the solicitors.

For a moment, at the mention of the jury, I felt my spirits sag. *Not Guilty. Not Guilty. Not Guilty.* It was branded onto the backs of my eyeballs; gouged onto the lining of my brain. I was disheartened, but more than anything, I was physically exhausted. I couldn't remember the last time I had slept properly. *Not Guilty. Not Guilty. Not Guilty.*

But then, my gloom was punctured by a sudden and hilarious reminder of Yousef racing alongside our car, trying to outrun us, every time we left the house. I could see him on the pavement, arms pumping, legs stretching, his big smile betraying his attempts at serious determination. Yousef was never out of energy. Yousef was never out of ideas.

"We don't have to accept anything," I replied hotly. "We need to fight for what is right."

Despite the attempts to dissuade us from campaigning, I left the meeting feeling even more determined. I was ready for battle.

"They're worried about what we're planning next," Mazen said, as we took the tram back home. "They want us to stop. They don't want to help us at all."

He was voicing my own thoughts. At least I knew, now, for certain, that I was on my own. My inbox was filled with requests from the media and, with that recent no-show of support from the police or CPS, aside from our wonderful family liaison officers, I accepted each offer. The following day, Mum and I appeared on Good Morning Britain and also on The Victoria Derbyshire Show. We spoke to various newspapers too. Mostly, as we answered questions, we managed to remain dignified, calm, proud. *'Jade you need to loosen up! You're on telly! Get some selfies!'*

But one interviewer asked us:

"How do you live without Yousef?"

The question was so enormous, so distressing, that I felt myself breaking down in a torrent of sobs, and beside me, Mum was shuddering with grief too. There was no answer. No way forward. We could not live without him. We could only exist.

Mum eventually said: "As a mum, every parent knows you will fight for your kids whatever and we never expected this to happen to us as a family so for as long as we're all alive, we will carry on.

"Yousef was a good boy, he was far from a gangster. He was into his sports, his basketball, loved boxing. Very, very kind – he was just such a popular boy. Everybody liked him."

The interviews were demanding and difficult, but they were a necessary tool for publicising our campaign. I was intent on toughening myself up and growing a harder outer shell. Something told me I was going to need it.

25

Only two days after the sentencing, Maz took me aside to show me a video on his phone. I knew, from his worried expression, that something alarming had happened.

"I got this today," he said, his voice wavering. "I don't know the person who sent it to me, but it was obviously meant for me."

I watched, uneasily, as a short film began to play, of Joshua Molnar making stabbing gestures and gun signs. The clip showed him thrusting forward his left hand, fingers clenched to suggest a knife, and shaping his fingers to represent a gun. There was a background of drill music which referenced 'shanks', a slang term for a knife, and included the lyrics:

'Two flicks in my hands, let's see who bleeds; back dem blades, put a dag in them, like the Heath; we come with shanks, they breeze.'

I felt absolutely sickened. Who in the world would be twisted and warped enough to make a video like this? And who would send it to Maz? Then, as I peered closer at the footage, I gasped:

"I recognise those floor tiles! Those are the toilets inside Manchester Crown Court!"

I had spent long enough in there over the past four weeks, locking myself in a cubicle to let the tears flow, before splashing my face with cold water and returning to court. The clip was definitely filmed in there. We checked the date on the recording and sure enough, it had been made during the trial by Joshua Molnar himself but sent to Maz by someone unknown. When I looked back over my notes from the trial, I realised the recording was made on the very same day that Joshua Molnar had been giving evidence in court. He had cried tears of apparent remorse under cross-examination. And on that same day he had made a video of himself performing stabbing gestures in the toilets.

"Why?" Maz asked helplessly. "Why would anyone do that?"

I found Joshua Molnar's lack of empathy completely incomprehensible. And I could see that Maz was, quite naturally, frightened and unsettled by the video too. He blinked back tears and I felt a sharp blast of fury. Maz was just 15 years old. He had lost his brother in horrific circumstances, and he'd sat through the unimaginable stress of a murder trial. And now this.

"Why me?" he asked again. "Why am I being targeted?"

I couldn't explain it. No decent human being could. I only knew that Yousef's death, and the results of the trial, had left me angry and scared and out of my depth. This wasn't like me, and this wasn't the person I wanted to be. Yet I felt as though everything I had once trusted, everything I had held dear, was falling to pieces around me. I was untethered, like a long kite string, unspooling, unravelling far more quickly than was safe. I was going to lose my footing. I watched the video again, the revulsion sloshing over me once more, and I no longer felt as though I was on solid ground.

"We have to do something about this," I said to Maz. "It's absolutely disgusting."

That same day, I sent the clip both to Greater Manchester Police and to the trial judge, Mr Justice Simon Bryan QC. I knew, from my own time at the trial, that it was illegal to take photos or videos inside the court buildings. The police confirmed they would launch an investigation to determine whether an offence had been committed under the Malicious Communications Act.

"So what happens now?" I asked. "I want to be able to tell Maz that someone will be punished for this."

"Leave it with us," they said.

But although I followed up my complaint, some weeks later, I was told there would be no charges made at all in relation to the video. It seemed to go unchecked and unpunished. In frustration, I requested a meeting with the police, and they again confirmed that no action was being taken. For me, it was hardly a surprise. I'd seen how the justice system worked and my expectations were, by now, at somewhere below zero. But Maz was a different matter. He was a child, a traumatised child, and he needed to know that there were systems in place to look after him.

"How am I supposed to explain this to my little brother?" I asked.

With nothing to lose, I spoke to the local newspaper, expressing my shock and anger. I didn't want it to be shoved under the carpet, and for Maz to feel as though his trauma was meaningless.

Matthew Claughton, from Olliers Solicitors, who represented Joshua Molnar, said in a statement in the press that the video clip was intended 'as a private message' for his girlfriend and 'does not reflect a lack of remorse on his part'.

Mr Claughton said: "It reflected his frustration with the way the prosecution were misrepresenting videos that were played at court. It's worth remembering that the jury appear to have agreed with that view given the not guilty verdicts.

"It will come as scant consolation for Yousef Makki's family but my client knows he will have to live with the consequences of that day for the rest of his life."

To me, the statement was contradictory. It was a nonsense. But then, nobody seemed to care how I felt, how Maz felt or how Mum felt.

"We have to put this behind us and move forwards, for Yousef's sake," I said to Maz. "I'm sorry."

As part of my work to kickstart our campaign, I had contacted a long list of solicitors and barristers, and the barrister Matthew Stanbury was the first to reply to me. He told me he'd seen Yousef's story in the press and wanted to offer his professional help in our fight for justice.

"Thank you," I said. "But I'm not sure we can afford your fees."

"I don't want payment," he replied. "Don't worry about that. I will work for free. I feel so strongly about this."

I was stunned. My faith in humanity had been shattered with the criminal trial, but now, with people like Matthew

Stanbury, and the hundreds who attended the protest, I felt a nascent surge of belief and the green shoots of hope. With such kindness and support around us, surely we could fight this? Maybe we could right this wrong? Matthew's first suggestion was to apply for leave to appeal against the defendants' sentences. Then, he advised, we would look at applying for a full inquest and also launching a civil action, the latter of which would be very costly. He suggested we could start up a funding page online, towards the costs of the civil case.

"Oh no," I said immediately. "That's not our sort of thing."

But he explained that we would need in the region of £100,000 for a civil case, and that online funding would probably be our only way of securing the money. Mazen and I promised to think it over, but for days, we were very unsure. We didn't want to be seen as grasping or begging and we didn't want our lives and our problems laid bare for all to see.

"But of course, our lives are already out there," Mazen pointed out. "We've started a campaign for justice. If we mean what we say, we need to raise funds somehow. We can't let our pride stand in the way of our campaign."

I knew he was right. But it was a decision we made with a heavy heart.

The funding page immediately attracted support and we raised thousands in a matter of weeks. We also attracted over 1,500 followers. I created 'Justice for Yousef Makki' pages on social media, which gathered over 3,000 followers. Again, it gave me a little bit of hope that there were people, like us, who thought that Yousef deserved better. But along with the support came, inevitably, ruthless trolling and mindless vitriol. A few days on, I was scrolling through the comments on the 'Justice for Yousef Makki' Facebook page and my blood suddenly ran cold.

'Three boys, three knives!'

'Live by the sword, die by the sword.'

'Go back to where you came from! You don't even belong here!'

'One less on the streets. What's the problem?'

'I blame the parents. They need to keep an eye on their kids.'

I hid my face in my hands to stop the children, who were playing next me, from seeing my tears. I couldn't bear to read this diatribe, but neither could I bear not to. How could anyone be so cruel? I had turned to social media for help, not abuse, but it was fast becoming a faceless vessel of spiralling hate.

"I'm not going to let them go unchallenged," I vowed, already tapping out my replies.

I didn't want confrontation or argument. I simply wanted to educate these trolls and hopefully win them round. But I found myself entering into long and twisty online discussions, explaining that there was no evidence at all that Yousef had a knife, save the evidence from two boys who were trying to save their own skin. Yousef had dabbled in cannabis, and he was an impressionable and immature teenager who had made some bad choices. He was hardly living by the sword.

'Back to where we came from?' I wrote. 'Do you mean

Burnage, in Manchester??? Yousef was born in Manchester, I was born in Manchester, so what is your point?'

But I soon realised that I was wasting both time and energy arguing with keyboard warriors who, no matter what I said, would simply reply with more utter rubbish. This was an argument I would never win because they constantly changed the goalposts.

"We just have to learn to ignore them," Mazen said.

We didn't let the trolls stop or even affect the campaign in any way. It was becoming more and more important for me to speak out – for Yousef, and for all the other children who had died as a result of knife crime.

'If nobody speaks out, nothing will ever change,' I wrote on the campaign pages.

The trolls continued to whine but over time they became like warts; small inconveniences that we just had to learn to live with.

26

A month on from the sentencing, Mum decided that she and Maz would remain living in the ground-floor flat in Chorlton, which was close to the cemetery and so of course close to Yousef. Mazen and I were therefore officially accepted as the new tenants of the old family home. It was a bittersweet moment; I was both looking forward to the move and dreading it too. I was trapped in a strange and contradictory whirl of wanting to be close to memories of Yousef yet finding them unbearably painful. On moving day, one of Yousef's best friends, Yas, came to help us carry boxes and lug furniture up and down the path.

"I miss him every day," Yas told me sadly, as we carried Daniel's highchair and baby toys out of the car and into the house. "It never goes away."

The children all helped out with the move too; thrilled with the promise of a new house, happily oblivious to the sombre connotations. There was a contrary feeling of belonging in sitting in my old living room and sleeping in my old bedroom. I could see and feel Yousef everywhere, and at times, I felt so close to him. I could almost smell the Lynx deodorant, hear him giggling in the hallway or swearing softly as he realised he had missed the school bus – again! The shadow-boxing hole was still there, in the living room door, and I was so pleased that Mazen hadn't ever got around to fixing it.

"We'll keep that hole there forever," I vowed.

The boys called it: 'Uncle Yo-Yo's boxing mistake.'

It kept him alive in their minds too. I loved going over these memories in my mind; I held onto them. Sometimes, I felt like I was drowning in grief, and I clutched the reminders to me like a life raft. But other times, in the dead of night, I pictured Yousef bleeding to death alone, in a strange street, and my memories threatened to pull me under. When I slept, I had that same recurring nightmare of Yousef grinning at me and refusing to answer me when I told him that I couldn't accept he was dead. Each time, he was wearing the clothes he had died in. Those white trainers were as vivid and as bright in my dreams as the day he had first pulled them out of the box. And the blood which seeped from under his black bubble coat felt so warm, and triggered such panic in me, that I could not believe that it was only a dream, a figment of my troubled subconscious.

"Yousef, please," I pleaded. "Answer me. Tell me that you're not dead."

And then I woke, and the cold and sober knowledge that he would never again answer me was crushing in its finality. I had another dream too, in which Yousef actually spoke:

"I will stay with you until you feel it's time to let me go."

But though I had longed to hear his voice, the words cut through me, sliced me open and left me sobbing and screaming in agony. When I woke, the pillow was soaked with my tears.

"Never," I whispered. "I can never let you go."

The two little ones, Zack and Daniel, moved into Yousef's bedroom and though a part of me wanted to keep it as a shrine to his memory, I knew that it was better to fill it with laughter, with noise and with life. Besides, practically, we had to use the space. There were five of us in a three bedroomed house. And the only other option – too painful to contemplate – would have been for another family to take over the tenancy. Yousef's belongings were still in the loft, his imprint was on every room in the house, and on all of our hearts. We had to stay here, we had to make it work.

"I love sleeping in Uncle Yo-Yo's room," Zack announced. "I can see him at his desk. I waved at him and he stuck out his tongue."

Later in the summer, our application to appeal the sentencing on the grounds of undue leniency was refused. The Solicitor General Michael Ellis QC MP refused the request officially in August. In a letter to our lawyer, Matthew Stanbury, Mr Ellis said in his view the Court of Appeal was "unlikely" to interfere with the sentences imposed.

He expressed his condolences but said after giving the case "the most careful consideration", there is "no evidence to suggest that he [the judge] fell into gross error during the sentencing exercise".

He said Adam Chowdhary's sentence did not fall within the unduly lenient sentence scheme, but he had reviewed it anyway and concluded it was unlikely to be considered too lenient.

"I am very sorry to Yousef's family that I am unable to give them the news that they will have been hoping for," he said.

It was disappointing, but not at all surprising. I was now slowly coming to expect that the establishment would try to block us at every turn. And if anything, that knowledge strengthened my resolve.

"We fight on," I said firmly.

'See! I told you. You can do it. There's an iron will hiding in there.'

We turned our attentions instead to campaigning for a full inquest into Yousef's death, where, potentially, witnesses would be called and questioned, and a jury would be required to reach a verdict. But it was another challenge. Another fight. We met with our barrister Matthew and also the Coroner for Greater Manchester South, Alison Mutch.

"The decision will take some time," we were told.

Misconduct investigations against the police's handling of Yousef's death were launched, for both Greater Manchester and Cheshire Police, but later dropped.

Then, in September, I got a call from our family liaison officer.

"Adam Chowdhary is being released from prison," she said. "I thought you would want to know."

Dizzy and weak, I folded into a chair. I was disappointed with myself for letting him get to me like this. I had known this was coming, after all. He had served half of his four month sentence in custody and the second half would be served on licence in the community.

I was not vindictive or vengeful. No sentence would

ever bring Yousef back, nothing would ever come remotely close to our agony. And I certainly didn't want other young men's lives to be ruined in prison.

Yet at the same time, it felt, once again, as though Yousef did not count. And now that the initial custody period was over with two months of the community sentence to follow, it only seemed more pathetic. It felt like Yousef's death had been almost incidental. An inconvenience, like a minor illness, a sprained ankle perhaps, which could be resolved and forgotten within a couple of months.

The release day dawned, and I felt physically sick. Poor Mum was even worse.

Two weeks before Yousef was stabbed to death, Adam had slept over in our family home. Mum had tiptoed into the living room, in the early hours, to check on his well-being and cover him with a warm duvet. Now, he couldn't even manage to compose a text to say: 'Sorry.'

I know he had expressed his contrition to the court. I know the family had been advised not to contact us, but I just wanted some personal contact. It was only human of me to crave that. I felt that we had not simply been forgotten or even deserted but viciously and deliberately trampled into the mud.

There was, of course, no possibility that we would bump into Adam Chowdhary and his family. We inhabited completely different worlds. And again, the geography was weighted in his favour, not mine, because I would have welcomed the opportunity to see him and speak to him.

I have to admit that I struggled to make sense of and

rationalise my own feelings much of the time; I know that the judges had accepted that Adam's regret about what had happened was sincere, but I wanted more from him. I didn't want to lose touch with someone who had been Yousef's best friend. He had been a big part of Yousef's life and I didn't want to cut him out. I felt sure he must be hurting and grieving, as all Yousef's friends were.

Adam Chowdhary's release from custody was all the more distasteful because a few weeks later, on September 28, Yousef would and should have marked his eighteenth birthday. As the date loomed closer, my throat was tight with anxiety and trepidation. As well as managing my own grief, I worried how Mum, Maz, Raafat and the little ones would cope. I was concerned about Yousef's friends too. Normally, for his eighteenth, we'd have planned a party; our small living room crammed with teenagers and ageing aunties and uncles; Mum marinating spicy chicken and popping open family bags of chilli crisps, whilst her terrible '70s pop blared from the speakers, and Yousef and Maz cringed with embarrassment.

'Mum, turn it off! Who listens to this stuff?'

'It's classic pop. Better than the rubbish you two like!'

Nothing fancy. Nothing special. But oh, so special. So precious. I would have given anything at all for one last birthday with him. I could hear his voice so clearly in my mind that I felt, if I closed my eyes, he might just be there when I reopened them.

'Check out my hair! Do you think I'm looking cool? Do you like my new aftershave?'

His birthday dawned and we had all arranged to meet up at Yousef's grave; friends, family, and many of his teachers too. We took a picnic of his favourite foods, which was shawarma meat, spicy chicken wings, and cans of coke! In front of Yousef's friends and teachers, we managed to smile and put on an act.

By now, we had a small black oval headstone in place, which read:

'King Of Our Hearts
Yousef Makki
28 September 2001 – 2 March 2019.

Your smile brought so much joy and light into our lives,
But the light went out too soon.
You lived your life to the full, loyal, loving and true,
May you always keep on smiling,
And watch those still loving you.
Beloved son, brother, uncle, grandson,
cousin and friend to so many.'

On the top, by his name, we had a small picture of a crown, a heart, and a pair of boxing gloves. We laid out blankets on the grass and passed the food around as though it was a regular celebration, as though Yousef might be joining us at any moment.

'Hey, save me some chicken!'

But as we walked away from the cemetery, back towards Mum's flat, we all broke down. The grief almost flattened me, right there, in the middle of the street. The ache inside me, the pain I felt, was so strong I sometimes truly feared that I might die from it. As I slumped onto the pavement, I felt Mazen's arms around me, pulling me up as though with invisible strings. And then Zack's little fingers furled into mine, and he lisped:

"Come on Mummy. I'll look after you."

Somehow, I made it to Mum's. For the rest of the day, we lit candles and played Yousef's favourite music, and we remembered the good times. There were, mercifully, many of those. But there, always there, a shadow in the empty chair, was the spectre of Yousef's bloody and brutal death.

Following the trial, Yousef's blood-stained clothes, or rather, the clothes in which he died, had been released to us. He had been wearing his own long-sleeved grey top. But there was a The North Face bubble coat, and a pair of Stone Island Cargo pants, both far too expensive for Yousef to afford. We had presumed, since he had stayed over with Adam, he had borrowed his clothes the following day, the day of his death. The jacket had a vicious slash right through it, where he had been stabbed. Mum could not bear to look at the clothes, the fact that they belonged to someone who was by his side on the day when Yousef was stabbed was too much to take. It seemed too far-fetched, too lurid.

But again, we were dealing with our grief from different perspectives. For when Mum wasn't around, I took the clothes out of the plastic wrapping, spread them across the kitchen table, and studied them for hours. Perhaps I was looking for answers, perhaps I was hoping for a connection with Yousef. Maybe I felt, somewhat ambitiously, that I could anaesthetise myself to the horror of knowing that my little brother had bled to death in this outfit. But every time I looked at them, the pain seemed even sharper, even fresher. And if I stared long enough at the clothes, they would often take on a shape and a life of their own, and reassemble into an image of my brother, staggering down Gorse Bank Road, clutching desperately, uselessly, at his bleeding chest.

'You've stabbed me!'

I was trapped in a cycle of pain as raw as it was relentless. Yet I was drawn back to the clothes, like the video clips and the clothes in Yousef's wardrobe. Time after time, I spread them out on the table, and I immersed myself in grief.

Then, we were approached by a BBC show called: 'Crime: Are We Tough Enough' and asked if we would be interviewed and share the images of the clothes.

"Of course," I agreed.

If nothing else, I hoped that the bloodstains might serve as a warning to other teenagers, against the cavalier use of knives. And too, as a wake-up call to Adam Chowdhary and Joshua Molnar. There was so much blood. So much pain. All from one blade.

We learned, through the media, that a task force within Greater Manchester Police, The Violence Reduction Unit, would be receiving a £3 million boost towards tackling violent crime, including knife crime.

The unit was launched, in part, in response to Yousef's death. The cash injection was a good start. I hoped it would be used to educate children – and parents – about the dangers of carrying a knife.

With so much exposure in the press, I found that people began recognising me in the street and in the supermarket, which at first, I found very disconcerting. I was normally so reserved and private, used to going about my day as a mum and a carer, melting happily and anonymously into the crowds just like anyone else. But this campaign leader and justice warrior was a whole new me and I was not at all comfortable with it. As I waited at the cash desk in Aldi, people would say:

"Good luck, Jade. The justice system stinks. Your brother was a nice lad."

They were only trying to help, and, after all, we needed the support of as many people as possible. But still, I knew I'd never get used to such recognition. I'd walk home from the supermarket, weighed down both by my shopping bags and by this new and lonely reality, in which there was no Yousef and in which I was his appointed voice.

At the end of October, we were invited to attend a knife crime vigil at Manchester Cathedral. There we met so many other families whose lives had been decimated by knife crime. The stories were all too familiar, all too tragic. Mostly young men, they had left behind gaping and enduring chasms of grief.

"I don't eat, I don't sleep. I haven't been into his bedroom since he was killed," one mum told me.

Another said she had visions of her son, skipping up the path, and tapping on the kitchen window, to make her jump. There was no comfort in the shared suffering, but more a renewed determination that it had to stop.

The most powerful moment of the evening came outside the cathedral, when Mum read out the victim impact statement she had originally prepared for the trial. She had never had the opportunity to read it out in public before. As the grieving mother, as the family of the victim, she'd been given no consideration at all. Now, under a cold Autumn sky, and with the light of flickering candles, she made her speech. It was incredibly poignant and moving and left the whole crowd in tears.

Mum said: "As I reached the hospital I stood in front of the surgeon and he shook his head, I knew then that my son was dead.

"He had been found dead with no-one to help him. Unless you have been affected by knife crime you cannot understand the heartbreak. You cannot imagine how it feels knowing that you can't touch your child because he is a piece of forensic evidence.

"My boy, who I protected for 17 years and watched him grow into a loving, beautiful and intelligent young man, was never going to walk into my room again.

"Imagine as a parent knowing you would never see him graduate or have kids of his own or even talk to me again, as he often did. We are completely broken, all we can try and do is change things for our other children...

"We need to teach children this is not acceptable in our society and make them fear the justice system, not mock it. Every life is precious no matter where you come from or how much money you earn. Now we have to live without Yousef forever."

It was a measure of how far Mum had come in her grief – and a measure too of her determination to fight for her son – that she was able to make that speech. Afterwards, as we waited at the tram stop, I fancied I could hear Yousef, in the wind.

'Wow Mum! That told them! Well done!'

27

Just a few days after the vigil, we had a rare reason to celebrate, when a letter from MGS dropped through our letterbox.

"Yes!" Raafat yelled, running around the house, waving the letter. "I'm in!"

He had been accepted into Manchester Grammar School on a scholarship. Yousef's tutoring had paid off!

"Thank you," I murmured silently.

"I'm going to be just like Uncle Yo-Yo," Raafat told me proudly. "I want to be a bursary boy, just like him. I want to study Chinese, just like him."

I was delighted that he wanted to follow in Yousef's footsteps. But of course I had my concerns. MGS was a wonderful school and they had shown us nothing but love and compassion since Yousef's death. But if he hadn't attended the school, Yousef would no doubt still be alive. It was that simple. Then, I worried too that Raafat, like Yousef, might be seduced by the wealth and the privilege around him. Would the envy eat him up, or would he eventually squash it, as Yousef had? Perhaps my biggest worry was the pressure on Raafat following on from Yousef himself; it was a huge challenge, and they were big shoes to fill. I didn't want him to feel the burden of expectation, which came from us all, no matter how hard we tried to hide it.

"Are you sure?" I asked him, over and over. "Are you absolutely sure this is what you want?"

Raafat was certain. He wanted to finish what Yousef had started. And alongside that, he wanted the advantages of a top-class education. Like Yousef, he was studious and bookish. Like Yousef, he wanted to excel. I knew that the teachers at MGS would take good care of him, and I realised too that because of Yousef's death, I would always worry more about the boys, no matter which schools they attended, or friends they chose, or nights out they planned. Regardless of what Raafat did, or where he was, I would worry. But I had to let him go and let him follow his dreams.

"We'll have a party to celebrate," I promised him. "We're very proud of you."

In that same month, we were contacted by a reporter from *The Sunday Times Magazine* who asked if we would be interviewed. He arranged to visit both me and Mum, separately, and also spoke with our campaign members. Afterwards, I thought the interviews had gone well and that he would do justice to our cause. A few days later, the same journalist called me to say that Joshua Molnar was due to turn 18 and that they would be applying to name him publicly, a few days before his birthday, as part of the article. The following Sunday morning, I dashed out to the shop to buy a copy of the newspaper early. But, as I scanned the article, I suddenly froze and clamped a hand over my mouth.

"Look at this!" I gasped, handing the magazine to Mazen. "It's an interview with Joshua Molnar's mother. They have named him and there are photos too."

I read the article in disbelief:

'The fatal stabbing of a Manchester Grammar School boy in leafy Cheshire brought the scope of Britain's knife crime epidemic into focus. Today, the family of Boy A, the teenager who killed him, tell their story for the first time…

'In their first – and, they say, last – interview, his parents have told me of their family's distress at Yousef Makki's death, the traumatic aftermath and their recognition of the lifelong impact on Yousef's family and all those involved…'

The article described Joshua Molnar's mother as 'visibly distressed' and her face 'etched with pain.' And the reporter once again and quite unforgivably repeated the unsubstantiated claim that Yousef had a knife:

'According to Josh's evidence, Yousef already had his knife out when he was stabbed…'

It was all I could do to stop myself being physically sick. I felt completely duped and betrayed. I felt I'd been tricked into giving the interview because I would never in a million years have taken part in an article alongside the Molnars. My interview was scarcely mentioned; the focus of the article was Joshua Molnar. So did living in 'leafy Cheshire' and coming from a wealthy family somehow make the Molnars' viewpoint more important than ours? That's how it appeared to me.

Joshua Molnar's father claimed that Yousef had stayed once overnight at his home; if true, it was certainly news to us. Mum did not know the family; she would never have agreed to an overnight stay without first speaking to the parents. It was possible Yousef had lied to her because he knew she would not approve. Even so, the boys were hardly good friends, as had been claimed in court.

The reporter wrote that Joshua Molnar was not in education at the time of the killing. He had attended two private schools and then a comprehensive but had "been withdrawn by mutual consent" after he had been caught at school with cannabis. His parents knew he was smoking too much and were trying to encourage him to stop. At the same time, his parents said that in many ways Joshua Molnar was "no different than any other 17-year-old in the area!"

Joshua Molnar's mother claimed that the case had been traumatising for all the families involved. Speaking about the trial, she said:

"I found those four weeks incredibly traumatic."

"The difference is that our son is still alive," she told the magazine. "It's hard for us to think about the future, but at least we have the possibility of one. They haven't even got that chance."

I was spitting with furious indignation. Just as I had thought they could go no lower, the Molnar family had trumped me once again.

If Joshua's mother had a shred of genuine compassion for us, why was she giving interviews to the national media? Her son had killed our son. He was not guilty of murder or manslaughter, but he had stabbed him through the heart. And yet she was speaking out about *her* plight and she had the superlative arrogance and obscene sense of entitlement to think she could speak about *us* and *our* feelings in the same breath. Why? She did not know the first thing about us. She certainly knew nothing of our pain. Again, it felt like we were insignificant, too far down the food chain and the social ladder to be of any real importance.

For me, it was a gross error of judgement from *The Sunday Times* to offer a platform to the Molnar family and their error was further compounded by the sycophantic and slimy slant of the narrative. Later, I was told that the Molnars had actually hired a publicist to represent them; they'd hooked up with a well-known PR firm in Manchester. The whole shameless episode left me shell-shocked. Clearly others felt the same.

MP Lucy Powell emailed me with her support, and we arranged to meet with her at her constituency office in Hulme.

"I will do what I can to help you," she promised. "But you don't live in my constituency, so my powers are very limited. But I will speak up when I can."

In Parliament, she described the death as a 'murder' and told fellow MPs 'his killers' were from affluent backgrounds. She contrasted the case with others where 'young black men from Moss Side' were serving life for murder.

She spoke of the 'burning injustices' highlighted in a government report into the justice system and asked in the House Of Commons whether ministers would address 'these very different outcomes in the same cases'.

Like any MP speaking in the Commons, her remarks were protected by parliamentary privilege, which meant she was immune from any legal action for what she said. Sadly, the same did not apply to us – Yousef's family. But we were eternally grateful to Lucy Powell, who seemed genuine and decent and driven by a quest for equality. Our own MP, when we tried to contact him, had failed to engage.

And Nazir Afzal, the former chief prosecutor for the north-west of England, tweeted about the interview in *The Sunday Times Magazine*: "This is offensive to the family of the boy that was killed. Can you recall the last time a killer (he's not a murderer) was given a page with a sweet picture to talk about why he did it? It smacks of white privilege."

I was glad that public figures and big names were lending their support and getting on board with the campaign. The poet Hussain and the rapper Alpha Riaz both sent messages of encouragement. I knew Yousef would have been so excited to have them fighting his corner.

'Hey! I'm famous! Just like I always told you! So sad I'm not there to see it.'

Christmas 2019 was fast approaching. But the prospect of facing the festive season without Yousef was like a sharp puncture wound into the delicate film which had begun to grow over my grief. I was dreading it. Without Yousef, there was nothing to celebrate. We were painfully aware however that we had to keep propelling ourselves forwards, for the sake of Maz and our three boys. Raafat was 10 now, Zack, two and a half, Daniel, 18 months. They were, like all children, so looking forward to Santa coming. Mechanically, I went through the motions of shopping, wrapping gifts, and putting up a Christmas tree. I strung lights across the room, around the hole in the door, and all I could think of was Yousef. It was traditional for Mum to cook Christmas lunch but this year, I offered to do it instead. She simply wasn't up to it. She was especially worried about Maz, who, after brightening a little over the summer, had now stopped attending school and was hardly leaving the house. He seemed to have lost all faith in the justice campaign; all interest in life.

He turned 16 early in December but had refused to celebrate the day and chose instead to spend it instead at Yousef's grave. We packed some spicy chicken, enough for Yousef too, and went to the cemetery in the biting cold and the rain.

Standing at the headstone, I could find no words to ease Maz's pain. He was suffering so much, and his mental health had plummeted. Any boy in his situation would be exactly the same. I remembered the stabbing video made by Joshua Molnar and sent to Maz by an unknown person and I felt a wave of hopelessness and despair washing over me. How could anyone be so cruel, so callous, so absolutely lacking in common decency? Maz was holding on. But only just. And that video had nearly pushed him over the edge.

"It will get easier," I said to Maz, as we walked back from the cemetery. "You will learn to live with this, in time. The pain will subside."

The words sounded so hollow and trite, and I wasn't sure I even believed them. But I said them, for Maz's benefit, to make him feel better.

"I know," he replied. "I know that."

But I sensed that he didn't believe that either and he was replying, for my benefit, and just to make me feel better. We were so wary, all the time, of upsetting each other, of leaning too heavily on each other. And in fact, each other was all we had. Family, as we knew all too tragically, was everything.

28

A few days before Christmas, we received a letter, from lawyers based in London, to say that Adam Chowdhary would be challenging the automatic loss of his right to anonymity, when he turned 18. I stared at the letter in absolute bewilderment. This was yet another twist of the knife, another stumble backwards in our grieving process.

"We can't afford to fight this in court," I said wearily. "And yet why should he hide behind anonymity?"

It seemed to me that Adam Chowdhary did not deserve to be granted this special status. I spoke to the police, who said they were not at all surprised by his application.

"I think the media will oppose this," our liaison officer said.

Next, I spoke with various newspapers, including *The Manchester Evening News*. They all assured me that they would be launching a joint action, opposing Adam Chowdhary's application.

"You don't need to cover the costs, that's our job," they said.

In the early days, following Yousef's death, we had seen the media as the enemy; trying to creep up on us and catch us out. Now, we worked with them, in a mutually beneficial relationship. I was glad of their advice and encouragement. Aside from the betrayal by the reporter from *The Sunday*

Times Magazine, I had found the journalists I encountered to be honourable and honest. Many of them were personally supportive of the campaign. We made a statement, explaining why we opposed the application, but with Christmas looming, we tried not to dwell on the letter. Even so, it lurked in the back of my mind like a malignancy. The fact that Yousef wasn't even here to enjoy Christmas, and Adam Chowdhary would be with his own family, was bad enough. But it stung even more that he wanted to remain anonymous and out of the public eye.

Mum and Maz arrived early on Christmas morning, and we painted on fake smiles, each afraid of saying what was really on our minds. The children tore around the house, trying on roller-skates and new footy shirts and leaving half-opened chocolate Santas to melt on the carpet. Yousef's ghost was everywhere; I could see him opening socks and pulling a jokey frown, I could smell his new hair gel, I could hear him helping my boys to build their new Christmas Lego. *'Pass me a red piece, one for the roof!'* Those memories were a comfort and a curse in equal measure.

'Not turkey!' I heard him complain. *'Why can't we have spicy chicken for Christmas dinner? Why can't I have a kebab?'*

Somehow, we made it through Christmas and the New Year. Adam Chowdhary turned 18 in January and the anonymity order elapsed, and he then lost a High Court bid to keep his identity secret for a further two years. The family's right to appeal the decision expired in February and he was publicly named. It felt like a victory, but a very small one. His legal team had argued he was suffering post-traumatic stress disorder and that publication of his identity would be 'catastrophic for him' and that he would be forced to move school.

But, dismissing his application, Mrs Justice Steyn ruled that: 'the curtailment of the claimant's and his family's right to respect for their private and family life is, in my judgement, clearly justified by the compelling public interest in open justice'.

Mrs Justice Steyn referred to his genuine remorse and added: 'The most significant aggravating feature was that (Chowdhary) bought the knife with which Yousef was killed.'

She said possession of a knife 'is a serious offence and there is a strong public interest in knowing the identity of those who commit serious offences.'

Mrs Justice Steyn found that 'the prospect of being named in court, with the accompanying disgrace, is a powerful deterrent' to others.

She added: 'There is an important public interest in understanding the prevalence of knife crime. Such understanding depends, at least in part, on knowing who is committing such crimes.'

Whilst I was relieved that the ruling had, for a change, gone in our favour, I was appalled that Adam Chowdhary's lawyers had referred to the disruption in his education. Where was Yousef's right to an education? And what about Maz, who was suffering from severe stress and hadn't attended school for weeks? Their selfishness, even now, was breath-taking. *'And he was supposed to be one of my best friends.'*

And yet there was little time to take the decision in,

because just two weeks later, Joshua Molnar was released. Though we had known it was coming, it was still like a high voltage shock, right through our family. It felt so incredibly unjust. Joshua Molnar had been found not guilty of murder or of manslaughter. Yet he had admitted holding the knife and killing Yousef. I could not reconcile those two issues in my mind, and I was tormented by the juxtaposition: Yousef had been stabbed to death. Joshua Molnar had been acquitted.

One week on, we marked the first anniversary of Yousef's death. We missed Yousef all the time, so the anniversary was no easier or harder than any other day. But the date represented a linear measure of our anguish, a box on the calendar, a quantifying of our suffering. For 365 days, we had been without our beloved boy. But the concept of time now seemed so unreliable, so twisted. The days no longer felt equal or equidistant, instead they bled into one another, seamlessly, with one crushing disappointment after the next. It seemed at once a matter of moments and a geological era since Yousef's death. It was both the blink of an eye and a hundred thousand years since he had dashed out of the house that Friday afternoon:

'See you later!'

Had he checked his hair in the neighbour's car window? Had he got a seat on the tram journey to Hale Barns? Had he enjoyed one last meal of takeaway chicken before his death? I didn't know. There was so much I didn't know. Our old life felt like a sweet and ephemeral dream; a halcyon paradise, as perfect as it was unreal. I missed everything; the awful rap music blaring out of Yousef's room, the eye-roll when he was asked to wash the dishes, the sickly scent of cheap aftershave catching at the back of my throat. Oh, I missed him so much. Whilst I had resolved to be strong for Mum, and for the children, I could feel myself splintering and cracking mentally. Those same dreams came almost every night, where Yousef was grinning at me and not speaking, and wearing the same clothes he died in.

"I won't accept that you're gone," I told him fiercely. "Give me a sign."

But there was no sign, and he did not speak and every time I woke, my heart broke all over again. Some nights, I just didn't go to bed at all; severe exhaustion was preferable to nightly terrors. My routine with the children never wavered. But though I was cooking healthy meals for them, I couldn't bring myself to sit at the table and eat. Instead, I'd comfort myself with chocolate or junk food or I'd pick at leftovers from their plates. I barely did any exercise, save running around after the little ones.

'You need to eat properly! Sport and nutrition! Trust me, I'm going to be a doctor.'

And even during the day, weak without sleep and proper meals, I had waking nightmares; I'd catch sight of Yousef's bloodstained corpse out of the corner of my eye as I was hoovering the living room. I wanted to reach him. I wanted a connection. But not like this.

"Maybe you should get some help," Mum said to me gently.

I nodded miserably.

I saw my GP who gave me anti-depressants and offered me counselling.

"It's no surprise that you're suffering, Jade," she said. "You've been through a lot."

Afterwards, I picked up the prescription and went home but something stopped me from taking the first anti-depressant pill. I filled a glass of water, popped a tablet out of the blister pack, and then, for some reason, I hesitated.

'Not yet, sis. Give it a few days.'

Perplexed, I flushed the tablet down the toilet. For now.

For the first anniversary of Yousef's death, we had organised an event, to raise funds and the profile of the campaign. The evening was held at Hotel Football in Manchester, which stands in the shadow of Old Trafford football ground. Yousef would have loved that, as a Manchester United fan. *'Get me some selfies with the players!'* They had kindly offered us the use of a room for free. Andy Burnham, the Mayor of Greater Manchester, agreed to speak. Rowetta, from the Happy Mondays, offered to sing. Yousef's teacher from Ladybarn Primary School gave a speech, saying:

"He continued to inspire the children around him. All the children wanted to be like Yousef, he wasn't just academic, he wasn't a geek of a child, he was a complete all-rounder, from music to singing to sport and as well as all the academic stuff, Yousef was the one who stood out. When I think about what you would want to have to succeed, Yousef had all of those things. He was charismatic, he had the presence of a child much older than his years, he would walk in a room and hold an audience, but he was always really humble, thoughtful, and caring. The staff would always want to teach Yousef, they were always impressed by him."

And his teacher from MGS spoke too:

"I met Yousef when he turned up to my History class ready to start his GCSEs... I couldn't help but immediately warm to Yousef's open and engaging personality, so much so that after teaching him for two years I asked if I could work with him as his form teacher in sixth form.

"The Yousef we will remember was extremely bright and intellectually curious. Despite that cheeky smile he was unfailingly polite and well loved and respected and a true gentleman. Academically he did excel and each year his report was filled with comments about his enthusiasm, his determination, and his ability. That Yousef had enormous academic potential was always evident. He didn't just want to know the simple answer to something...

"The Yousef we will always remember was an incredibly caring young man; he gave as much back to the school as he took out of it. The written tributes from younger boys will always stick in my mind. Yousef had been supporting younger ones without having been asked to, without being part of any formal scheme, he did it just because he wanted to help. From getting involved in the Duke of Edinburgh Award Scheme, tennis, basketball, even chess, winning silver in a national Maths challenge and performing in the Shakespeare festival, Yousef threw himself into the opportunities around him. But what made him stand out was that he wanted to say thank you. He had a serious side too. He worried about doing well..."

As I listened, I felt the pride and the love pouring out of me. Yousef had made an impression on so many people. He'd had such a great future ahead of him, which was what made it all the more tragic for him to be taken from us so cruelly.

Many of his teachers and friends came to the anniversary event. But the most honoured guests as always were the families of the victims of knife crime, those people, like us, who were life-long members of an exclusive club that none of us wanted to belong to. For me, it was a chance to talk about Yousef, to see his photos on the walls, to remember the boy he was and the man he should have become. But for Mum, it was still so raw and sore, and probably always would be. She managed to get through the anniversary but again, it was a challenge and a trial. She would never get used to talking about her son in the past tense. What mother ever could?

The day after the anniversary, I called round to check on Mum and Maz and she looked at me shrewdly and said: "You have the 'tired eyes' again, Jade. I think you're pregnant."

I smiled and shook my head. Her sixth sense was usually uncannily accurate; I knew that from past experience. But this time, I was sure she was wrong. Mazen and I were happy with our three boys and were not planning any new additions. Even so, after enjoying a coffee with Mum, I picked up a pregnancy test on my way home.

"Just to be on the safe side," I said to Mazen, and he smiled.

Sure enough, she was right, and it was positive.

"No!" I gasped. "I don't know how she does it!"

This was, incredibly, my 13th pregnancy. I must have been only just pregnant on Yousef's anniversary. In that moment, I knew that if I was carrying a boy, I would like to call him after my brother and Mazen agreed. I had been asking Yousef for a sign, for a link to him, and I felt strongly that this was it. He had sent this baby for us, as a chance for us to smile and feel love and happiness again. Mum and Maz and everyone around us was so pleased by our news and I knew that this little miracle, heaven-sent, was already working his magic.

"I know you're a boy," I whispered, with one hand on my stomach.

'Correct! He's a boy – a fourth nephew for me and Maz!'

As with my other pregnancies, I was very sick in those early weeks and had to be monitored carefully. I tried hard not to let the stresses of the campaign get to me, worried that it might affect the baby, but it was asking the impossible.

'I'm watching out for you and the baby, stop stressin'!'

And soon after, the country was plunged into strict lockdown, and neither Mum nor Mazen was allowed to attend hospital scans with me. It was odd going to appointments on my own, but I felt mostly for Mazen and Mum, who were missing out on the excitement. Instead, I booked a 3D gender scan some weeks ahead, for June 5, so that I could bring home a video for them to see.

"If the baby is a boy, I'd like to call him Yousef," I said to Mum. "But only with your blessing."

I wasn't sure if the suggestion might upset her. But she

turned to me, her eyes shining with tears, and she nodded her head.

"I think that would be lovely," she replied. "And I think Yousef would be thrilled, really honoured. He will live on in all of your children."

I checked with Ghaleb too, and his response was the same as Mum's.

"Thank you, Jade," he said. "It's a wonderful idea."

All through April and May 2020 we visited Mum and Maz two or three times a week, driving to their flat and parking outside, so that they could wave from the window. In their front garden was a little apple tree, planted in memory of Yousef. My boys were so close to Mum and Maz, and they all cried and clamoured to get out of the car for hugs. To my children, their grandmother was 'Mum' and I was 'Mamma.'

"Mum!" they shouted. "Uncle Maz! Come outside! Can we sleep over?"

They didn't understand the concept of lockdown at all. And even through the window, I could see that Mum looked pale and fragile, older than her years. From the road, she looked almost transparent, and I told myself that it was just a trick of the light. But I worried more and more about her, mentally and physically. I knew that Maz was the only reason she got up each day and continued with her life. But she didn't complain; that wasn't her way at all. She did her best to look forward.

"When lockdown is over, I'm going to throw a big party for you all and for Yousef's friends," she told me on the phone. "I might do a barbeque if it's sunny. The kids can sleep over here, give you a break, Jade. Oh I've missed them so much!"

She sounded more like her old self. But I knew it was all an act. I knew she would never recover from losing her son. What mother ever could? On May 15, it was Zack's third birthday and, after driving to the cemetery to see Uncle Yo-Yo, we drove round to Mum's later in the afternoon. She had left gifts for Zack on the doorstep and when we had collected them, she came to the window to wave at the children. But seeing her just made them cry with frustration.

"We want to go and see Mum for a sing-song and a sleepover!" Raafat pleaded. "Please."

I sighed and shook my head.

"Soon," I promised. "Just as soon as we're allowed. But not yet."

The next morning, I sent Mum a daily WhatsApp as usual, and she replied to say she wasn't feeling well.

'Maybe it's the heat, affecting my arthritis,' she said.

I agreed. It was very warm, and the weather often made her illness worse. We swapped more messages, but she was a doting granny and was more interested in finding out how the boys were rather than focussing on herself.

"Raafat is enjoying home schooling," I replied. "But the other two are running riot. They're going stir crazy, shut in the house all day."

That same evening, Mum messaged to say she was having an early night. The next morning, I couldn't get hold of her, which was unusual. I tried calling Maz instead.

"She's still not well, I tried the doctor but they're busy," he told me. "She's getting worse, not better. I'm worried about her."

"Let's get an ambulance," I decided.

But Mum wouldn't hear of it. She didn't want a fuss.

'I'm fine, don't over-react,' she told me in a message.

I had anticipated that she would be against the idea of going into hospital. She had, since Yousef died, missed many of her hospital appointments, because she could not bear to set foot inside the building. Hospitals brought back the traumatic memories of the night of the stabbing. As a result, her condition was not well monitored and could be a little more unpredictable than before.

"Ok, no hospital," I agreed.

We managed to get a doctor out who confirmed that her arthritis was indeed flaring up and he left her with some medication. But by the next night, Maz was so concerned that he called an ambulance. Mum was by now too ill to object. Maz messaged me just before the paramedics arrived.

'You did the right thing,' I replied. 'They'll treat her with stronger tablets in hospital and she'll be home before we know it.'

Mum was admitted into Wythenshawe Hospital, but we were not allowed to visit because of Covid restrictions. Stuck at home, I felt so powerless. We were completely in the dark.

And I was worried about Maz too; he had been through so much already and now he was completely alone at home in the middle of a lockdown. We couldn't even go and see him until Mum had been tested for Covid. I had to be extra-careful because of my pregnancy.

"I'm fine," he insisted when I called.

"You sound like Mum," I laughed.

But in the meantime, Rachel had travelled up from Devon to be with him and she arrived that same night. We all believed that Mum simply needed a short course of treatment for arthritis and she would be allowed back home again afterwards. I texted her and she replied to say that she was very tired, but that we mustn't worry.

"Typical," I said to Mazen. "She won't ever focus on herself."

The following day, a doctor from the hospital called and announced that Mum was being taken into the Intensive Care Unit.

"What?" I stuttered. "Are you sure? What's wrong with her? Is her arthritis that bad?"

But she was being treated for possible sepsis. We were warned she was deteriorating quickly. I tried calling and texting her but by now she was too ill to reply.

"We're going to lose her," I said tearfully to Mazen. "I can feel it."

Knowing that her time was running out, Rachel and Maz were allowed to go to the hospital, to be with her in her dying moments. I waited anxiously at home for the Covid test results. The moment I got the call to say: 'Negative' I jumped in a taxi.

By the time I arrived at the ICU, it was shortly after 4am.

"I'm sorry," Rachel sobbed, meeting me in the corridor.

"She passed a few minutes ago." I felt myself go weak. I had missed my chance to say goodbye.

My mum, my best friend, and the kindest person I knew, was gone. She was just 55 years old. All through her life she had battled against circumstances which would have floored many people, but not my mum. She'd survived poverty, domestic violence and broken relationships. She'd lived in a Texas mansion and a homeless hostel. She'd raised four kids on her own and we could not have asked for a better mother. She'd met each obstacle with a smile on her face; she saw it all as an adventure. She was one of a kind.

The doctors told us that her death was caused by sepsis, but we all knew with total certainty that Mum had died from a broken heart. Right from that first minute, when she heard of Yousef's death, she had been counting down the moments when they could be together again. For her, the adventures and the smiles stopped when Yousef died. Her only purpose on earth had been to look after Maz, but her body had not been as strong and resilient as her spirit. The nurses told us that Mum had been calling Yousef's name before she fell unconscious.

"I hope she can see him. I hope they're together now," I said sadly.

Back at home, I wondered how much stress and loss one family could possibly take. Some days, I felt as though we were being singled out to suffer. First Yousef, now Mum. Yet I felt strongly that the two deaths were linked; this was no tragic coincidence. News of Mum's passing spread quickly and staff and parents from the primary and secondary schools asked if they could pay their respects. Rachel organised the funeral, at our local Catholic church. Mum had found her faith a great crutch since Yousef's death, and we knew she would want a Catholic service followed by a burial. Yet over the years she had insisted that when she died, she wanted us to have a big party.

"No crying and no moping about," she always told us.

Mum's favourite song was: 'I'm So Excited' by The Pointer Sisters. That summed her up perfectly. Truth was, I had never felt less like partying. Despite my growing baby bump, I felt hollowed out and empty inside. The grief was gnawing away at me.

We were allowed only 10 people at the church but along the way, neighbours and friends and the children's teachers lined the streets and clapped as her coffin passed by. Mum had touched so many people with the way she had fought for her son, right to her dying breath. The words of her victim impact statement, read out so courageously at the vigil, came back to me:

'You cannot imagine how it feels knowing that you can't touch your child because he is a piece of forensic evidence.

'My boy, who I protected for 17 years and watched him grow into a loving, beautiful and intelligent young man, was never going to walk into my room again.

'Imagine as a parent knowing you would never see him graduate or have kids of his own or even talk to me again, as he often did.

'We are completely broken.'

Mum's heart had stopped beating because it was broken.

On that fateful night in Hale Barns, when Yousef was stabbed, two lives were lost and many more were destroyed. She had limped on, after that first devastating blow, but inside, she was withered and fatally wounded. Just over a year on, she had finally succumbed. She was finally at peace.

"Goodbye, Mum," I whispered. "And thank you."

After the church service, Mum was buried in the same cemetery as Yousef, in the Catholic section. I had slipped a scan picture of our unborn baby into her hands, inside the coffin, along with a photo of my three boys and Maz. She and Yousef were close enough to have a conversation, and for her to reach out to him. But she was also far enough away not to have to listen to his dreadful music!

'Banter! Mum we can have a chat and a bit of a dance if you like?'

My only comfort, as we walked away from her grave, was that they were now together, looking after each other. It was a beautiful day, warm and bright, and it felt like a betrayal. I wanted the heavens to weep with us. Mum's death had crucified us all.

Already, in those first few days, the children missed her and pined for her. Raafat had chosen not to attend her funeral, because of the trauma he'd suffered after seeing Yousef in his open coffin.

"I'd like to remember her just as she was," he told me. "The sleep-overs we had, the cakes she baked, the silly dancing she did around the kitchen."

Zack asked her for every day, searching the house, calling her name, just as he had when Yousef passed away.

"Mum!" he yelled, which was what he had always called her. "Mum, where are you?"

Once, I heard him giggling, all to himself, and he told me: "Mum is tickling me! She's here now and she's tickling me!"

Perhaps it was just his little-boy way of processing his grief, conjuring up ghostly images of Mum and Yousef. But I liked to think that it was more than that and the link was real. I missed her so much too; she and I had been the best of friends as well as mum and daughter. Her greatest gift to me was to teach me how to be a mother. With my own boys, I followed her example, I copied her lead. Birthdays, especially, were a blow-out. But my heart hurt every time I thought of her.

Maz, especially, was bereft; since Yousef's death, he and Mum had held onto one another, and they had relied on each other. Of us all, he was certainly the most dramatically affected by her passing for, now, he was left without his mother and without his home. Ghaleb by this time was living in London and though he visited sometimes, Maz wanted to stay in Manchester with his family and friends and near to his school. And Mazen and I both knew, the moment that Mum passed away, that Maz belonged with us. There was no question of him going to live elsewhere. It was a squash, especially with a new baby on the way, and not ideal for a teenage boy to be surrounded by exuberant toddlers who dived on his bed each morning, sticky with breakfast jam and refusing to let him have a moment's peace. But I knew also it could be therapeutic to distract Maz from his sorrow and keep him busy with the little ones. I wanted to keep him close, where I could look after him and make sure he was loved. It was what Mum would have wanted; I was certain of that.

"It's what I want as well," Maz said, and I held him tight.

And living with us, Maz formed a closer bond too with Mazen, who became, as he had been with Yousef, a father-figure. Mazen helped Maz choose his A-level subjects, and together they began looking at universities and courses online. The kids loved having Maz living with us; he and Raafat shared a bedroom and that made Raafat feel very grown-up and mature.

"Me and Uncle Maz both talk about politics," Raafat told me, seriously. "I'd like to be a doctor, same as Uncle Yo-Yo, and Uncle Maz might be a politician."

I smiled. All children deserved a childhood. All children deserved a dream.

After the lockdown ended later in the summer, Yousef's friends began to visit us again, and one day, Yas called round wearing the MGS Leavers Hoodie.

"Look at the back," he said. "Tell me what you see."

On the back of the hoodie, as is traditional, was a list of all the boys in that year group. As I scanned the names, I suddenly squealed with excitement.

'Yousef Makki!' I exclaimed.

He was there, along with all the rest, all his friends. It brought tears to my eyes. MGS had included him on the list, without question, as one of the boys. Adam Chowdhary's name was not on the hoodie, and I understood that he had not been welcomed back at the school after the court case.

The A-level exam results were announced, and Yousef's friends all celebrated on social media. I was thrilled for them all; genuinely thrilled. But in my mind's eye, I could see Yousef, sloping in through the front door with a long face.

'Failed them all. Got to resit. Won't get into medical school now.'

And then, just as Mum was sinking into an armchair in dismay, he let out a shriek of laughter and danced around the living room, yelling:

'Three A-stars! I'm off to Oxford! I'm going to be a surgeon and I'm going to buy you a new house, Mum!'

It was a daydream. A little fantasy. And nothing more. All that promise, all that potential, just wiped out and wasted with one single stab wound and one knife worth £2.

One by one, his friends went off to university for new adventures and new beginnings. Again I was so pleased for them all but each time I felt a ripple of regret for Yousef.

"This should have been you," I whispered.

I imagined him, packing his suitcase, ready for Oxford University, ready to study medicine. I truly believe he would have made it all the way to being a cardiothoracic surgeon, just as he had always wanted.

"I'll be in all the newspapers one day," he had promised us.

The irony was heart-breaking.

Another birthday rolled around, and this should have been Yousef's nineteenth. I was by now heavily pregnant and there were still some Covid restrictions in place. At home, we lit candles and played his favourite songs, and though I was determined to remember the good times and the happy memories, the tears flowed. I missed him. I knew

I'd always miss him. And this year, when we visited Yousef's grave in the afternoon, Mum was missing too. We let off 19 red balloons and the little ones enjoyed watching them bob and float through the graveyard until a gust of wind whipped them into the sky and snatched them agonisingly out of view.

"Goodbye Uncle Yo-Yo," they waved, and it was a blessing that they didn't understand at all the impact of his loss.

Visits to the cemetery and balloon releases were all they had ever really known. But for me and Mazen, and for Maz too, it felt as though this tragedy was picking off members of our family, one by one. We had taken snacks and a can of coke to the graveside, and I whispered: "Happy birthday, lovely boy."

It was bewildering to think that he would now be 19, almost a man. He had been a boy when we had lost him. The passage of time seemed relentless, heartless. It seemed not to care about us at all.

29

Later in October 2020, Raafat started officially at Manchester Grammar. In his uniform, as he posed for his first day picture, he looked uncannily like Yousef. And as we arrived outside the gates, I had mixed feelings; the place would always, in my mind, be inextricably linked to Yousef and his death. *'Let him go, sis. He'll be fine. He'll make the right choices, I'll look after him.'* Raafat was very excited. He had a new school bag, and he was using Yousef's own calculator and some of his pens too. Around us, the posh cars and the chauffeurs were arriving in some style. But I was used to that by now and unlike the first time, I was less than impressed. The first day format had changed and instead of going into the main hall for an induction, I left Raafat at the front door. I was so grateful for that. I couldn't have sat through a copy-cat induction, with the boys on the stage, with the same speeches, the same promises, the same goals. When Raafat came home that night he was bursting with enthusiasm.

"I have the same teachers as Yousef," he told me. "They're all there, all still there. They know he's my uncle and they showed me the memorial tree."

He had chosen to study Chinese too, just like Yousef.

"I'm going to China, just like he did," he babbled. "And don't say it's too far because really, I'll be fine."

I rolled my eyes. I thought back to Mum with the loan man, squirreling away every spare penny so that her golden son could enjoy the trip of a lifetime. I would be doing the self-same thing myself too. It would come around soon enough. *'Don't worry. And he'll be good at Chinese, I bet.'*

And then Mum added: *'You'll find the money, love, don't stress about it. Little savings make a difference, especially if you start now.'*

I loved hearing their voices in my mind, feeling them close to me. And yet, at the same time, they were horribly far away. Mum's advice was infinitely more practical and sensible than Yousef's but I relied on him to make me giggle.

As Raafat settled in at MGS there were times when I needed to pop into the school, perhaps for a special assembly or to drop off a PE kit he'd forgotten. Sometimes, I loved going to school; I longed to go, because I felt I could almost touch Yousef. His face and his voice and all the memories I held dear, cascaded over me like warm and healing water. I stepped inside the entrance hall, and I drank them in. *'Come and see my old classroom. And this is the library.'*

But there were other days when my grief would get the better of me, and I could not bear to set foot inside the school. Just looking at the entrance hall would remind me of the decaying shrine of flowers and letters from the pupils. In my mind's eye, I'd see a hazy apparition of Yousef in his uniform, standing at the end of the hallway, dripping in blood.

'He stabbed me!'

It was such a huge achievement for Yousef to get to MGS. He was such a brave and ambitious and maverick boy. He had reached out, far outside his own comfort zone and grasped each opportunity with grateful hands. He had, in truth, reached for the stars and he'd got there too. Yet it hit me, each time I went to the school, that his education, along with his life, had been snuffed out as quickly and unceremoniously as a flickering candle. He had fallen, cataclysmically, from the brightest star.

Raafat joined various sports teams and when I saw the price list for his kit, my eyes watered.

"A hooded top for £44.75!" I shrieked. "A games jersey for £45.50! Where will we get the money for these?"

Even a simple base-layer, for outdoor games, was over £30! I was familiar with high school PE kit prices, because Maz had just left school himself. And his kit had cost a fraction of this. Once again, I felt keenly the worry and the dilemmas that Mum had faced.

'It will all work out,' she reassured me again. 'You could try the second-hand swap shop and you should have a look through Yousef's old clothes in the loft too; there may be a PE kit in there. It'll be ok, you'll see.'

30

My pregnancy had been classed as high risk because of all my miscarriages, and so I was being looked after by a specialist department at St Mary's Hospital called The Rainbow Clinic. I had scans every two weeks and towards the end, I had weekly checks. Strangely, I felt no anxiety. I felt sure that Yousef and Mum were looking after me and the baby. I was booked in for the birth to be induced on November 5, but in the days beforehand, I could feel my body getting ready and I knew, instinctively, that our fourth son was on his way. Mazen and I went to hospital, and Rachel came all the way from Devon to look after the kids whilst we were away. Again, I was so grateful to her; there was a geographical distance between us, but since losing Yousef and Mum, she and I had been so close.

"I owe you one," I said, as I puffed out of the door with my hospital bag. "I promise this is my last baby too!"

Checks showed that I was 2cms dilated and in slow labour.

"No need to be induced after all," smiled my doctor.

I'd had caesarean sections with both Zack and Daniel, but I was eager to try for a natural delivery this time and my doctors were very encouraging. But frustratingly, the labour was so slow! I paced the corridors at the hospital, and I even tried a slow jog to get the baby moving. I bounced up and down on the large rubber balls in the maternity ward until I was dizzy, but nothing happened. Rachel sent spicy food and curries into the labour ward, but they didn't work either! Mazen wasn't allowed to stay in hospital, because of Covid restrictions, until my labour progressed.

"I need you to come out," I told my bump sternly. "We have to get home to your three brothers and your Uncle Maz!"

Three days on, my waters finally broke and the pains came thick and fast. Mazen was called back to the hospital, now that I was in full labour, and I gripped his hand as each contraction tore through me. As I yelled and panted, my midwife peered at me and said:

"I recognise your face from somewhere, have you been on the telly?"

I blushed in embarrassment.

"Well, yes," I replied. "But I was thankfully fully clothed on that occasion!"

She was extremely interested in Yousef's story and outraged at what we had been through. As my labour entered the final stages and I began to push, I felt as though I had no more energy left. Then, through half-open eyes, I caught sight of Mum, shimmering and glowing at the side of the room, as though she was lit up from within. Her smile, aimed right at me, was dazzling.

'You can do this, come on love,' she urged. *'You're about to meet your baby boy. Come on now, breathe, breathe, push.'*

Six minutes later, our son, Yousef, came into the world. He was absolutely perfect and weighed 6lbs 5ozs. He would be cherished and beloved by people from this world, and from the next.

"Meet your new nephew and name-sake: Yousef," I whispered.

'Ah, he's handsome like me, too.'

The kids made such a fuss of baby Yousef when we were allowed home. He looked just like his big brothers, but he had a strong look of his uncles too. There was a thread running through them all and I loved that. Baby Yousef's arrival gave us all a reason to smile, to numb the pain a little.

"Thank you for our new baby," I said to Yousef, the next time I visited the cemetery.

'Welcome! Now, have you got £2 for boxing?'

I was in no doubt that Yousef had sent little Yousef to save us all. And it had worked perfectly. Christmas came soon after, and again, the children pulled us through the day. We had a bauble made with Yousef's name on it, and the children squabbled over who would hang it on the Christmas tree.

"I'll do it for him," Zack said firmly. "I told him I would. I saw him yesterday. He was here to charge his phone."

I smiled. Zack's little meetings with Yousef, however fantastical, made him happy. Christmas Day itself was very tough. I remembered the previous year, Mum unable to face cooking Christmas lunch, her face creased with grief and despair. We had thought then that life could not get any worse, without Yousef. This year, I looked at Mum's empty chair and I felt a swell of longing.

'*Happy Christmas,*' I whispered.

I hoped, and believed, that Mum and Yousef were both together; Mum's benevolent ghost tutting good-humouredly at the way I basted the roast potatoes, Yousef's moody teenage ghost groaning at the Christmas jumper I'd bought for Maz.

'*Bro, you can't wear that!*'

The New Year of 2021 brought fresh anguish, a harsh reminder, not that any was needed, of what we had lost. But I wanted to look forwards too and I gave thanks for my four lovely boys who kept me afloat. Each time I felt as though I was slipping under, and I could not cope, something seemed to happen to pull me up and keep me going. Sometimes it might be just a funny little quip from one of the children, or maybe I'd get a message from one of Yousef's friends, sharing an old memory. And one day, Yousef's old primary school got in touch, to give me just the lift I needed on a grey day. Ladybarn Primary school were announcing the creation of The Yousef Makki Award, to be given annually to an all-round achiever, in and out of school, in his memory. It would be voted for by teachers and governors.

"We wondered if you might come into school to present the award at the end of the academic year?" the teacher asked.

"Of course," I agreed. "Absolutely, I would love to."

I was humbled by the support of the school and honoured that Yousef's name would continue to shine. His legacy in education would outlive all of us and that seemed very fitting, for a boy like him. I had a sudden flash to Yousef as a little boy, asking if he could go to school at weekends, and pleading with the teachers for extra homework. Even at the age of four, Yousef's spiritual home had been inside the classroom. I imagined fondly that he was there still. I thought of his work, hanging on the wall in the classroom at Ladybarn, and realised that he lived on in many ways, and in many hearts. I hoped The Yousef Makki Award might inspire children to push themselves, not just academically, but outside of the classroom too.

We were also granted permission to create a small memorial to Yousef at the tree where he died. One of the local residents was Nigel Martin-Smith, the former manager of boyband Take That, and he helped us with the application to the council, and also gathered support for the memorial from the Hale Barns neighbourhood group. He even insisted on paying for the plaque, bearing Yousef's name and dates, himself. It was another example of the kindness of strangers; another reminder that most people are good at heart.

31

After a long and costly campaign, an inquest into Yousef's death was confirmed, scheduled towards the end of 2021, and we began to plan and to hope. Then in the days beforehand, we were hit with a setback.

In September 2021, a pre-inquest hearing was told Cheshire Police had referred itself to the Independent Office for Police Conduct (IOPC) over their response to 'incidents prior to the death of Yousef Makki,' and the police watchdog's final report had only recently been completed. Lawyers for Joshua Molnar, and also for the police, wanted time to consider the report. These were the first rumblings and I steeled myself for more bad news.

In October, Mr Molnar's lawyer, Alexander Leach QC, argued there had been 'no fresh material' in connection to Yousef's death and said a full inquest was not justified. He referred to charges Joshua Molnar had faced over handling an iPhone stolen in a violent robbery weeks before Yousef's death, although there was no allegation that Molnar was involved in the mugging. Molnar was handed a 12-month conditional discharge for the offence at Chester Crown Court, three months before the pre-inquest hearing.

Mr Leach QC told the hearing at South Manchester Coroner's Court: "No fresh material has arisen about the circumstances leading to the death of Yousef Makki.

"We submit there is no longer a sufficient case for the resumption of this inquest.

"There is no link between the offence on February 17, 2019 and the night of Yousef Makki's death. It is no longer proper for this inquest to continue."

Our lawyer, Matthew Stanbury, urged the coroner to continue with the inquest and we were sent away to await a final decision. We faced days of anxiety, feeling as though we were left dangling from a string, relying once again on a stuttering justice system to keep us from crashing to the ground.

One week on, at the end of October, we got news that the inquest would go ahead as planned on November 8. It was a victory for us. I was under no illusion and had to accept that the hearing would be as much about closure as justice; I was by now cruelly aware that the two are not necessarily the same thing. At the request of the coroner and in line with standard practice during the pandemic, we were told Joshua Molnar and Adam Chowdhary, along with their legal representatives, would appear via video-link only. Mazen and I chose to attend in person. It was a huge disappointment for me that I wouldn't get the opportunity to speak, face to face, with the two men who had the answers to all the questions which had tortured me for so long.

The weekend before the hearing, I rushed out to Primark

to buy some cheap smart clothes; a black and white shirt and black trousers. I arranged for friends to help with the school-run and to look after baby Yousef. Monday morning dawned, and I felt sick with anticipation. It felt so odd; in many ways this was a re-run of the build-up to the criminal trial, but of course Mum was missing now. I was doing this for her, as well as for Yousef. And as I brushed my hair in the hallway mirror, I could feel them both with me, Mum complimenting me on my make-up, Yousef edging me out of the way so that he could admire his own reflection!

"You should eat," Mazen insisted, coming out of the kitchen with a slice of toast.

"Can't," I grimaced. "My stomach is doing somersaults."

"I'm the same," he confessed, slipping his hand in mine.

Outside South Manchester Coroners' Court, we held up a framed photo of Yousef as a press pack snapped photographs and asked us questions. Outwardly, I was trembling with anxiety. But inside, I felt a sense of calm and pride.

That first day, I had agreed to speak on behalf of my family. All night, I'd been wide awake, worrying I might forget my words, panicking I might let Yousef down. But as I cleared my throat, and I looked at Yousef's smiling photo on the desk, I felt a warm blanket of reassurance and love, wrapping itself around me.

'You're not alone, sis.'

I thought back to the criminal trial, how we were not allowed to speak as we wanted, how Yousef was denied a voice. This was our chance.

"I don't think I have ever met anyone like Yousef,"

I said. "I don't think I will ever. He was a good brother. Good fun.

"He was a straight-A student, he was very, very bright. He could speak Mandarin and had ambitions to go to Oxford University, become a heart surgeon and find a cure for arthritis.

"I last saw Yousef alive the day before when he was full of energy, full of life like he always was. He was like the Duracell bunny."

There was some laughter in the court at that, and I imagined I could hear Mum and Yousef's voices, mixed in with the crowd.

'Stop embarrassing me! Enough now!'

Our lawyer, Pete Weatherby QC, asked me whether Yousef was ever interested in knives, had a 'hot temper' or got into fights, and I replied:

"He was a peacemaker. He was everything you would want in a brother or son."

'Peacemaker. Thanks, sis. Thanks for telling the truth.'

Just to be allowed to speak, to defend Yousef, after being so violently silenced at the trial, was an honour and a relief. At the trial, we'd been hidden away behind glass screens, like unwelcome and unruly guests. Here at the inquest we were sitting at a desk; we were being treated like humans. Some of the bitterness and the frustration, which had bubbled and festered for three years, was dissolving, and melting away.

Finishing, I said: "I had a baby last year and named him Yousef. I miss my brother every day. It's a huge void which we will never get back."

In the following days some of the key witnesses from the trial were called to give evidence. Retired detective Inspector John Mulvihill told the inquest he had attended the scene of the tragedy and had made the decision to change the status of Joshua Molnar and Adam Chowdhary from witness to suspect.

He said: "I went on to the street. It was a long straight road. The light was good... They were the last people to be with Yousef, prior to his death. It was a wide, straight road. It was difficult to comprehend how a knife attack could take place without either boy seeing or hearing anything given they were in close proximity to Yousef at the time."

Giving evidence via video-link, Joshua Molnar stood by the evidence he had given at the trial. His statement, prepared for the inquest, said:

"I stand by my evidence on oath in my trial. I tried to answer all questions honestly and to the best of my ability but, as I made clear, my memory as to the exact sequence of events was patchy.

"It remains patchy and I have tried not to think about it as it is very upsetting. I was a boy and the events, which left me totally out of my depth, were extremely traumatic. I deeply regret having initially lied to the police...

"We were boys playing stupid games, particularly in relation to knives, which led to an unnecessary and tragic death. Yousef was not any sort of gangster. He did not deserve to die."

Molnar told the inquest hearing he could not recall whether he or Yousef had pulled out a knife first and described the incident as 'a really small clash.' Adam Chowdhary, who had not taken the stand at the criminal trial, this time gave evidence in person at the inquest and insisted he did not see Yousef being stabbed and said: "I had no reason to believe that Josh was responsible for stabbing my best friend. The possibility had never crossed my mind."

He claimed that one of the two knives he had bought online was for Yousef. He said that Yousef and he had decided to buy the knives whilst they were in the school canteen and that Yousef had paid him cash for the knife. My blood boiled as I listened. I didn't believe it and, of course, Yousef was not here to defend himself.

It was a small comfort to hear from Adam some of the details of Yousef's last day; Adam's mother had made them a late breakfast, and then they had contacted Joshua Molnar and arranged to meet him. Hearing this direct from Adam was inconsequential to most people, but this was part of the picture I had been trying to build since losing my brother. I needed so desperately to know what Yousef had eaten that day, what he had said, how he had slept the night before.

Martin Bottomley, the head of the major crime review unit at Greater Manchester Police, told the hearing that Adam Chowdhary's phone was found in his mother's car (Adam was arrested as he got out of the car) and when it was examined, some of the data had been deleted at some point – it was not clear when – though some was later recovered.

After six days of evidence, the hearing was adjourned for a decision. Deep down, I held a glimmer of hope that our request of 'unlawful killing' would be granted. But it was a glimmer, and no more. Molnar's lawyers were pushing for a conclusion of 'accidental death' which I felt was appalling, but not unsurprising to me.

In her summing up, the coroner Alison Mutch said it was clear there was 'no evidence Yousef had fallen out with anyone' and that he was a 'contact point' between the two defendants. She said that the CCTV appeared to show Joshua Molnar taking Adam Chowdhary's expensive coat and that the former was 'annoyed about losing his bicycle'. Yousef 'played no role other than what appears to be a peaceful role' at that time, she said. 'Adam's evidence is that he and Yousef had together dealt with, ordered those [the knives]…' she added. 'Of course, Yousef isn't here to give us his account in relation to that.'

As she spoke, despite myself, I felt the hope growing within me. The coroner appeared to be endorsing and confirming everything we knew to be true. But announcing her conclusion, she said she could not consider unlawful killing as she could not be satisfied as to the precise sequence of events.

My stomach plunged. I felt as though I had been guided to the very top of the tallest of buildings, and, upon reaching the final step, I had been brutally pushed off, into freefall.

Ms Mutch said she had instead recorded a narrative verdict that Yousef died from 'complications from a stab wound, the precise circumstances of which cannot on the balance of probabilities be ascertained.'

The room swam before me, through eyes blurry with tears and a heart wounded by layer upon layer of setback and pain. Aware that the witnesses were watching via video, I stood up and walked calmly from the courtroom. It was only when I got outside, into the autumn gloom, that I allowed the tears to fall.

This time, unlike at the criminal trial, there was no chaos, no screaming, no outrage. Mazen sank down beside me, and a hurt silence hung between us. I felt empty and hollow. Physically, I was exhausted; I was on the brink. Mentally, I felt even worse. But I was certain of one thing; this was not the end.

As the verdict sank in, I questioned much of what had been said at the inquest and in particular Adam Chowdhary's claim that he and Yousef had been in the school canteen when they decided to buy the knives. I did not, could not, believe this of my brother.

December came, and with it, more controversy.

An internal report by Greater Manchester Police highlighted a string of failings by both Greater Manchester and Cheshire Police, during the murder investigation following Yousef's death.

The report described how, just a fortnight before the stabbing, Joshua Molnar was stopped in Wilmslow with a balaclava and linked to a knife. Cheshire Police arrested but then de-arrested Molnar after finding he had a balaclava on him – while drugs and a sheath knife were found in the taxi van in which he and other youths had been travelling. Molnar told officers he had the balaclava because it was 'cold'.

The report said the officer who was leading the 'stop search' in Wilmslow showed 'little appetite' to identify who in that group had possession of the knife and drugs – although he was captured describing the knife in the taxi as 'a bloody good knife'.

A second officer was recorded saying 'it's gone to pig s*** this job'.

Neither Cheshire Police – nor the GMP detectives who investigated Yousef's death just 13 days later – sent the knife found in the Wilmslow stop for forensic analysis.

The report was painful to read. If Joshua Molnar had been arrested and properly investigated at that time, Yousef would, I believe, still be alive today. Shameful too, that a serving police officer was recorded saying 'a bloody good knife.' What example is this to our young people?

After the inquest, our local newspaper, *The Manchester Evening News* made a successful application to the coroner to publish the CCTV footage which showed the moments leading up to Yousef's death.

The CCTV had been shown at the trial, but we had been stuck high up behind the glass screen and I had never seen it up close and in the correct sequence.

With a knot in my stomach, I watched the film of Yousef jogging down the street – towards his own death.

I wanted to reach out and grab him and pull him to safety.

"Stop!" I screamed silently. "Turn around. Come home to your family!" But he didn't stop. He didn't hear me. Yousef continued running.

Moments later, he was dying in the street.

32

Through the campaign I was contacted by many other families who had lost members to violent crime, often tragically without justice or closure. I spoke with the brother of Stephen Lawrence, the 18-year-old who was murdered in a racially motivated attack in London in April 1993. They had campaigned and fought for years for justice. I was also contacted by the family of Alex Rodda, a 15-year-old boy from Cheshire, who was murdered by 20-year-old Matthew Mason. Mason was handed a minimum life sentence of 28 years in January 2021 but it was later reduced to 26 years. His family was disillusioned by the justice system. There were so many tragic stories, so many lives decimated by knife crime. It made me all the more determined to continue fighting, not just for Yousef, but for every child.

We have found out, to our cost, that knives taint every section of society; even the richest, the brightest, the most fortunate. We need to talk to all children about knives, de-glamourise them and de-myth them, and show them the photos of Yousef's forgotten school-bag, his redundant boxing gloves, his blood-stained white trainers. We need to tell them the painful truth.

Official figures state that in the year ending March 2020, there were around 46,000 (selected) offences involving a knife or sharp instrument in England and Wales. This figure did not include data from Greater Manchester Police. In the year ending March 2019, there were 259 homicides using a sharp instrument, including knives and broken bottles, accounting for 39 per cent of all homicides. In the year ending June 2019, there were 22,306 disposals given for possession of a knife or offensive weapon. Juveniles, aged 10-17, were the offenders in 20 per cent of cases.

Knife crime feels like a tidal wave. The figures are astounding. I understand only too well the agony caused by one death from a knife, and yet this is being repeated in a pattern across the UK.

Despite everything, and it may surprise many people, I would still welcome a meeting with Adam Chowdhary and his family. Adam was one of Yousef's closest friends; he loved him, and he had so many good times with him.

The decision to buy knives online was one which led to Yousef's death. Yet I have no doubt that Adam is hurting too. I need to know about Yousef's last moments, I want to hear his last words, and however much it hurts, I have to know about the fear and the pain in his eyes. Surely Adam owes me this, at the very least?

Anger and blame are powerful emotions, and they are very heavy to carry around, each day. I would like to let them go. I want to forgive Adam, though I understand that not everyone will share my sentiment. If I have forgiveness inside me, can he find it inside himself to meet with me?

My intentions are genuine. My heart is pure. My door is open.

Joshua Molnar is more difficult for me to forgive. He pushed the knife into Yousef. He made videos glorifying knives and violence. He wept on the stand in Manchester Crown Court and then he made a video showing stabbing motions inside the toilets. I want to feel compassion for him. But I also want him to feel genuine remorse. Again, I would welcome a meeting with him and his family. No cameras. No glitzy PR firms. Just the truth.

We have recently requested a review of the inquest verdict, and we are still looking at the prospect of civil action. We need to raise £100,000 to launch a case, and our fundraising is ongoing but slow. I understand of course that we can't expect, we can only hope. Mazen and I also took part in a Channel 4 documentary about Yousef, which was screened in March this year.

Meanwhile, I'm a busy mum, with Raafat, now 12, Zack, four, Daniel, three and baby Yousef, who celebrated his first birthday in November last year. I am working hard on the campaign too.

Raafat is about to start Year 8 at MGS and so far, he loves it! I like to think his Uncle Yo-Yo is looking after him. He's already asked me if he can go on the year 9 China trip, as Yousef did, so I need to start saving up.

Maz is studying for his A-levels, he is applying for Oxbridge, and he hopes to study Philosophy, Politics and Economics at university next year. He's a brain-box, just like Yousef. Mum would be so proud of the strength of character, way beyond his years, which he has shown since her death. Mazen continues to work with troubled teenagers, hoping his intervention will prevent other lives being lost to knife crime.

I've stayed in touch with our family liaison officers and the paramedics who looked after Yousef. They've become friends, confidantes, over the years. I'm in close contact too with Yousef's former teachers, his friends, his sports coaches. Everyone wants to keep his memory alive. Everyone loves him still.

We visit the cemetery every Sunday to spend time with Mum and Yousef. Once, Zack picked out his favourite toy car, a red one, and said to me:

"Uncle Yo-Yo would like this."

I didn't think he would part with it when it came to the crunch. But I had tears in my eyes when he produced the car from his chubby little hand at the graveside, and shouted proudly:

"I've brought you a present, Uncle Yo-Yo. I hope you like it! Red for Man Utd!"

"He loves it," I beamed, wrapping my arms around him.

Yousef lives on in my head, every day. When I'm washing dishes at the sink, I see him sometimes. It might be just an outline of him, like a line drawing, without the colour and the texture filled in. It's ghostly and eerie yet at once such a comfort to me. Or he might be skipping:

'Can you count for me? I'm doing 300!'

Or he might be teaching Raafat to box:

'Jab, cross hook, come on, get the sequence right,'

Or he might simply be admiring his profile in the glass of the window pane:

'No wonder the girls love me, look at my hair!'

I hear him dashing out for the school bus, tripping over the shoes in the hallway, dropping a trail of crumbs from his toast. I smell his aftershave too; the cheap Lynx, or the expensive stuff he pinched from Mazen. He's all around me.

I've kept all the reminders of him around the house. His name is still there, scrawled on the back fence, and we have the basketball hoop, the boxing gloves, the football. We have a 'Justice For Yousef Makki' poster in our front window. His belongings are all around us, not as a ghoulish shrine, but for the kids to play with and enjoy and remember their Uncle Yo-Yo. And of course we still have the damage to the door. I will keep that forever. Who knew I could become so fond of a hole in the door!

Mazen has kept the cloth that he used to wipe the blood from Yousef's face, shortly after his passing. He carries it in his pocket every day. Maz has a silver chain which Yousef liked to wear, his signet ring, and his old footie shirt. I've kept his favourite Germany World Cup shirt, and also a hoodie which he wore a lot. I also have a little flag from China which Yousef brought me back from his Year 9 trip and the little ones enjoy waving that about.

When Mum died, I took ownership of Yousef's glasses, and we have all the rest of his stuff in the loft. Maybe the day will come when I feel it's the right time to get rid of it all, but I just can't see it. My most treasured possession is the pound coin from Yousef's pocket.

That solitary coin was with him when he died, it was in his pocket when his heart stopped beating. He had just one pound to his name, on a street in a millionaires' paradise. For me, it's so much more than a pound. It's priceless.

Every life is equally precious no matter where you come from or how much money you earn. Losing Yousef destroyed us, but the love he left behind has given us the strength to carry on. We will fight on for justice for the boy with the pound in his pocket.

Other bestselling Mirror Books

The Convent
Marie Hargreaves
With Ann and Joe Cusack

**When a fancy car pulls up outside six-year-old Marie's home
in Oldham, in 1959, she is told she is going on holiday...**

In fact, she is taken to live in a convent, overseen by a cruel
and sadistic nun. There, a horrific ritual of physical, sexual and
mental abuse begins.

Marie feels unable to share details of her suffering with anyone.
Until years later, when a police investigation is launched, and she realises
that the time has finally come to tell the truth...

MIRROR BOOKS

written by Ann and Joe Cusack

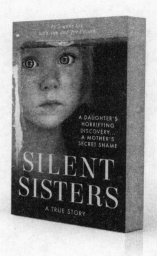

Silent Sisters

Joanne Lee

With Ann and Joe Cusack

A DEADLY SECRET. A HORRIFYING DISCOVERY.

**For over 20 years, Joanne Lee's mother kept the
remains of her newborn babies hidden in her wardrobe.**

Growing up in a chaotic Merseyside household, Joanne suffered neglect and
abusive control while her mother lapsed into a downward spiral. But the
consequences of her mother's messy lifestyle turned out to be far worse than
Joanne could ever have imagined – the family home held a sinister secret.

In Silent Sisters, Joanne, who was falsely accused of murdering her own
baby sister, tells her story for the first time – her struggle to piece together
the truth and to give four babies the proper burial they deserve.

MIRROR BOOKS

Other bestselling Mirror Books

The Asylum
Carol Minto

With Ann and Joe Cusack

Born into poverty and with mostly absent parents, Carol helped to raise her nine siblings. But when she was just 11 years old, her older brother began to sexually abuse her.

After four years, Carol managed to escape – and ran away from home. Picked up by social services they placed her at the infamous Aston Hall psychiatric hospital in Derby where she was stripped, sedated, assaulted and raped by the doctor in charge.

This is the full story of how she overcame unimaginable suffering, to find the solace she has today as a mother and grandmother.

written by Ann and Joe Cusack

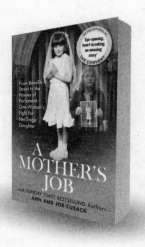

A Mother's Job
Joy Dove
With Ann and Joe Cusack

While Jodey Whiting was stuck in hospital battling pneumonia over Christmas, a letter dropped on her doormat from the Department of Work and Pensions, asking her to attend an assessment. It was a letter she never saw.

Despite suffering from major health problems, the powers-that-be callously halted her benefit payments. While waiting for her appeal, and with no money coming in, Jodey killed herself, aged just 42.

A Mother's Job is the story of how Jodey's mum Joy Dove, 67, took on the system – and won justice for her daughter.

MIRROR BOOKS